The Searchers

The
SEARCHERS

GUSTAF STRÖMBERG

Author of *The Soul of the Universe*
and *Man, Mind, and the Universe*

SCIENCE OF MIND PUBLICATIONS
Los Angeles, California

Science of Mind Publication edition
is published by special arrangement with
David McKay Company, Philadelphia, Pa.

Second Printing August, 1967

Copyright © 1948 by David McKay Company

All rights reserved, including the right to reproduce
this book, or portions thereof, in any form, except
for the inclusion of brief quotations in a review.

SCIENCE OF MIND PUBLICATIONS
3251 West Sixth Street
Los Angeles, California 90005

Printed in the United States of America

Dedicated
to
Sister Benediction

Contents

CHAPTER	PAGE
INTRODUCTION	ix
1. *Boris Charkoff*	1
2. *A World of Things and a World of Shadows*	13
3. *Gravitation*	27
4. *Expanding Waves and Small Particles*	46
5. *Vibrating Atoms and Exploding Bombs*	80
6. *Living Dust*	110
7. *The Roots of Our Consciousness*	138
8. *The Immortal Soul and an Almighty God*	163
9. *Conversation in a City of Sleepwalkers*	209
EPILOGUE	219
INDEX	241

Introduction

THE QUESTION whether or not the world is what it looks like has been asked by thinking men since time immemorial. To a primitive man, as to a child, the world consists of more or less permanent *objects*, like hard stones, high mountains, green fields, blue lakes, a solid earth, a bright sun, and many shining stars. There are also living things, like plants and animals and men, and these have many properties identical with those of the inorganic world. There are objects which can be used for food, shelter, clothing, tools, and weapons. Most men of the present time are *realists* who claim that the world is what it appears to be to their sense organs, and they are interested in action and not in speculation about ultimate things. Their philosophy is often the result of a struggle to satisfy their immediate needs, but instinctively they retain their general outlook even after these needs have been satisfied. They have no desire to look beyond the world of their direct experience, largely because they doubt that there is anything worthwhile to look for. They may or may not be satisfied with their world, but in general they are busy working in it, enjoying it, and perhaps improving it.

There are also men of another type who regard the material objects of the realist as fleeting *phenomena* in their own minds. Plato was perhaps the first to give these ideas a systematic form. His philosophy was characterized by a certain contempt for a knowledge directly derived from our senses. The real world is not a world of matter, but a world of *ideas*. Our mind is able to discover and to study this world behind that of our sense perceptions, because our soul, that is, the personality behind our mind, is born with a true knowledge of fundamental realities. This knowledge is in a subconscious form, but by intellectual efforts, stimulated and aided by observations, we can bring it up to the level of consciousness. Then, and only then, do we know something about the real nature of the world and about the meaning of our own lives.

The conflict between these opposing views, between materialism and idealism, has gone on for many centuries. On the pages of the history of philosophy we find the struggle described as one between the dogmas of many conflicting schools of thought. In the history of ethics we find on the one hand the idea that ethics is nothing but practical man-made rules of conduct in an organized society, and on the other hand the idea that ethical values also represent an intuitive recognition by our conscience of eternal laws that cannot be violated with impunity. The idealistic conception of the world has been given explicit recognition in religious philosophies and creeds. These creeds often contain a statement that man has an immortal soul that has come from God and returns to Him at death. Materialistic philosophy in the occidental world reached its culmen during the last century when it had its most outspoken proponent in the physical science of that time. According to this science, the world is built of atoms and of configurations of atoms. But we know that matter acts at a distance, as evidenced by gravitational and electrical fields of force capable of doing certain amounts of work. Since in this science there could be nothing but matter, a field of force must itself be material, and therefore there must exist some subtle form of matter, imperceptible to our sense organs. This tenuous form of matter was called "ether," and one of its principal purposes was to serve as a medium to carry light waves from one place to another. It was later found that certain phenomena were completely incompatible with the idea of a stationary ether, and then the Theory of Relativity was born. The most important consequence of this theory was that matter in general contained an enormous amount of energy, a prediction that was verified in a spectacular manner when part of this hidden energy was released in the atomic bomb. When the ether concept was dropped, it became necessary to define fields of force in terms of their action alone, with complete disregard of any mechanical models. Gradually it was realized that science describes effects rather than causes, and that the intrinsic nature of the world is not the subject of physical research.

The materialistic concepts have thoroughly permeated the biological sciences. Living organisms are supposed to be built of atoms and act as machines, although of extreme complexity. Fields of force appear during the embryonic development of animals, but most biologists still hope that some day the physicists will discover or explain the relationship between matter and its associated field. Then these "organizing fields" can be regarded as the effects of inherited chemical substances transmitted to an individual by the germ plasm. This hope of the biologists has not been realized. On the contrary, recent discoveries indicate strongly that a field of force, both in inorganic and organic matter, is a primary cause rather than a secondary effect. All fields of force appear to be *autonomous*, that is, they are independent of the elements of matter involved, and they arrange the material elements in a pattern in accordance with the inherent structure of the fields.

In the first year of the present century leading scientists all over the world were startled by an event of the greatest importance. This event was the discovery by Planck of the *Quantum of Action*, a discovery which led to the realization that nature does not work according to the simple rules they had envisaged. Events occurred which showed that energy could not be indefinitely subdivided. Light sometimes acted as if it consisted of waves and sometimes as if it consisted of small moving bullets containing the full energy of the emitted light. The electrons, which had been regarded as small, electrically charged particles, were found to be associated with wave systems. And always the mysterious quantum of action was found to regulate the elementary physical events. This caused scientists to scrutinize the extent and nature of the knowledge they had derived from their measurements. A new world then began to appear, a world of mathematical symbols, where space and time do not furnish a scaffolding wide enough to co-ordinate physical measurements, and where the future is not completely predictable from our knowledge of past events.

The greatest mystery confronting scientists is still the old problem of the relationship between mind and matter. This mystery involves the problem how we are able to think at all, how our will can cause mechanical effects in our muscles, and how we are able to remember past events. Here we approach a fundamental problem that is directly connected with the ultimate origin of our thoughts, the existence of a universal mind—and of a God. The question of the immortality of the soul is also directly involved in this problem. With the disappearance of mechanical models and concepts, old philosophical problems appear again, although in a new and scientific form.

The two antagonists, Metaphysics and Natural Science, have met on a common field of research, and the result has been a greatly extended field of vision.

In discussions of the kind presented in this book many facts and theories must of necessity be described in a cursory form. On account of the extreme importance of the problem of the immortality of the human soul, the scientific arguments bearing on this problem have been brought together in an *Epilogue*. Interested readers may find a detailed and systematic description of the scientific facts and their interpretations in the second, revised and enlarged edition of the writer's book *The Soul of the Universe*. In this edition six articles written by the author during the last five years and published in various scientific magazines have been reprinted. Although these articles were intended primarily for scientifically trained readers, they were written in such a form that the average reader can profit greatly by studying them. Some historical data and references to the modern scientific literature are there given.

Pasadena, California
September, 1946.

CHAPTER I

Boris Charkoff

BORIS CHARKOFF was walking the streets of New York. He had arrived a month earlier as an immigrant from Russia with great hopes for the future. His father had taken an active part in the awakening of the Russian masses and in the great development during the leadership of Lenin and Stalin. Boris had seen much suffering and sacrifice during the war, when his country was overrun by a ruthless army bent on conquest, but he had also seen a great devotion to a new order. He had been a soldier in the war, but he was a sensitive man and wanted to forget many of the incidents from this period, when the life of the individual counted for so little.

He had come to America at the urgent request of his uncle, a prominent Russo-American in New York, who wanted to use the talented young man in his business, the nature of which Boris did not know. His uncle had influence in Moscow and had succeeded in securing emigration papers for his nephew when the fighting had stopped. Boris' father had been killed during the siege of Leningrad, and his mother had died when Boris was very young. His uncle had no children, and now he wanted Boris to help him in his business and perhaps later take it over.

When Boris met his uncle they soon got into a heated argument about some advertising work which the older man wanted him to do. Although Boris was an ardent communist and wanted to promote the interests of his fatherland, and certainly had no use for religion, his innate sense of right and wrong was so strongly developed that he could not participate in giving out statements which he knew were not true, a practice he had been told was very common in the capitalistic countries. Boris and his uncle were both proud and headstrong men who never compromised with their convictions, and a break was inevitable.

"Go ahead and make your own living," his uncle said. "You may come back when you are starving, then, I think, you will look at things in a different way."

"I intend to make the best of my life. And don't count on my coming back," said Boris. And he left without a handshake, his head raised high in a defiant gesture.

Boris did not doubt that he could shift for himself. In fact, he was proud of having an opportunity to show the world how a worthy son of the modern Russia starts his career in the New World. He had a very good education. He had studied several years at the University of Leningrad, where he was regarded as a brilliant student, and he had made good marks in engineering and social economy. He could speak English very well, and understood a little French and German, but he had no knowledge of the classical languages, which he considered of little use in the modern world. He was a good singer, and he played the violin with great skill and feeling. He was exuberant with energy when he considered the work he was doing worthy of his effort.

The practical men at the University said he had one great fault. He was an introvert who pondered over the meaning of life, and he would rather talk about the significance of scientific facts than about the methods of applying them for the benefit of his countrymen. He had the making of a philosopher, but he would angrily have protested if anybody had insinuated that he might belong to this group of useless, unrealistic people. He had just shown that he had a conscience but, if somebody had told him so, he would vehemently have proclaimed that a conscience was an invention of the priests and the landowners to secure the good behavior of the proletariat.

Usually Boris was very happy and seldom took a very serious view of life, although he had his moments of melancholy. It was probably his artistic and philosophical nature which showed up in these moments, and then he became very pessimistic and bitter. This time he was particularly depressed, because his money was almost gone, and he knew that, if he did not pay his rent tomorrow, he would be evicted by his landlady. She had told him that she was a Christian and she went to church regularly, but Boris had ridiculed her religion and could hardly expect any special consideration. Besides, she could easily get another tenant, and she needed the money to pay her own expenses.

He walked slowly up Broadway and stopped at all the shop windows. Strange how many things you could get in a capitalistic country, if you only had the money. America is a wealthy country, he said to himself, but Russia has the raw materials to produce all these things, and her people are more willing to work for the common welfare than are the Americans, who only work for themselves. In a few decades the great scientists and engineers in Russia will surely make it the best place in the whole world to live in. For myself, he said, I do not care much where I live. I am a citizen of the world, and my field of action is as wide as the whole world. I do not want to make a great fortune and live on other people's work. I want to be a useful citizen and not a parasite. If I had a little money, I would write books and show the Americans the folly of capitalism and religion.

Boris had little more than a dollar left in his pocket and no idea where to get any more. He had been looking for work, but without success. He was too proud to beg or to ask for any special favors from the few countrymen he knew in the big city. "Darn these capitalists! Here I am, a strong, talented man, who can do much useful work, but nobody seems to want me. If I were in Russia, I would offer my services to the government and they would gladly give me work."

He felt hungry, however, and after a little hesitation he went into a small restaurant and ordered a sandwich and a cup of coffee. He ate his meal slowly and listened to the conversation around him.

Strange people, these Americans, he thought. The girls had painted their cheeks, lips and finger nails. They were fairly good looking, no doubt about that. He had heard that during the war some of them worked in the factories, but he could not imagine them doing hard work on a farm or fighting among the men, as many Russian girls had done. The men around him seemed to be most interested in gambling on the races or on the stock market. They could be greatly excited about a horse race or a baseball player, as if the destiny of the world depended upon what horse or what team should win. Some talked about getting higher wages by going on a strike. Others spoke about politics and criticized the government freely. In Moscow before the war people of their class used to talk about art, the latest play in the theater or opera, co-operative farms, or new scientific discoveries. He admitted to himself, however, that they did not dare openly to criticize the government.

Having somewhat satisfied his craving for food he continued his walk. He came to a store where they sold Russian books and propaganda literature, and he went in. The clerk whom Boris engaged in conversation was a Russian. Did he know where Boris could find any work?

"What kind of work do you want?" asked the clerk.

"I can work in a machine shop or help in a drafting department," said Boris. "I can contribute to magazines, sell books, or play in an orchestra."

"I know a Russian who is playing in an orchestra at a dance hall on Broadway. He is well acquainted with musicians of all kinds."

Boris went to the dance hall and asked for the musician, whom he found to be an old man with a kind face. He was given an opportunity to show his ability on the violin. The old man was much pleased and wanted to know about Boris' knowledge of music in general and learned that he was well qualified as an instructor in music.

"Are you a member of the union of musicians?"

"Of course not," said Boris. "I have heard that there is free competition in this country, and the devil takes the hindmost."

"I cannot then at present help you with any job as a musician, but I will recommend you to a music teacher who may need assistance."

The old man wrote something on a card and sent Boris to an institute for musical teaching. Again he had to demonstrate his ability. The director was quite satisfied with the young Russian's performance and asked him to come back the next day when he would try him out as an instructor.

So began Boris Charkoff's career as a music teacher in New York. There was little money in it, but he had enough for living expenses. In the evenings he often went to concerts conducted by great masters, many of whom were Europeans who lived in or visited the great metropolis.

Boris was an industrious student of everything in the great city. He went to museums, libraries and lectures. He talked to all kinds of people, and soon he learned that behind their flippant talk there was much serious thinking, although most people disliked discussions about the fundamental things in life. He discussed religion with many of his friends, but they were either not interested at all, or fanatical believers in some particular brand of religion. Some even said that, if you did not subscribe to their faith, you would suffer eternal punishment. He went to churches and saw statues of the Madonna with the Child and people bending their knees before the image. We did that in Russia not so long ago, he thought, and many ignorant peasants still do it. We used icons which the priests showed to the congregation and carried in processions. If we have to have icons, I would rather see Lenin's picture than Christ's. And we don't pray to Lenin's picture, we merely honor his memory.

Boris went to churches of many different denominations. In some there was an austere atmosphere and many ceremonies. In others there was singing and shouting, and the people seemed really happy and said they were saved. From what, he wondered. He went to the Salvation Army and Father Divine's meetings, and he appreciated their efforts to bring all races together and to alleviate human suffering and bring happiness to despairing souls. This he understood, but he did not see why it must be associated with a belief in a Supreme Being or in a life after death.

One day Boris was hurt in an automobile accident and went to a doctor for treatment. The doctor was a Jew named Paul Berman, who also was a psychologist and philosopher, an outstanding member of that great race which has made so many contributions to the intellectual and moral development of mankind. Boris used this opportunity to engage the doctor in conversation about science and religion, and Berman realized immediately the outstanding qualities of his patient. He lent him a copy of Spinoza's *Ethics* and asked him to call again.

Boris read the book with astonishment. He learned that Spinoza had tried to demonstrate that behind the world of appearances there was an immutable essence or substance, and that everything was a modification of or an emanation from this transcendental substance. The God of Spinoza was immanent everywhere, in atoms and stars, in hills and brooks, in plants and animals, in his flesh and his bones, in his eyes and his ears and, above all, in his own mind.

This was a revelation to Boris. It was a God that appealed to his scientifically trained mind and cool intellect. It was not a God to be loved or feared, not one amenable to supplication or flattery. He himself was an actor in a cosmic drama, the meaning of which was beyond human understanding.

At first Boris was in exultant spirits. He thought he had solved the riddle of the universe. His new God was far superior to the idols the savages worshiped and to the God spoken of in the churches. The new God did not care if ignorant men believed in him or not and certainly did not punish men for their ignorance or reward them for their faith in him.

After the novelty of the new vision had worn off, he began to wonder. Was he really nothing more than an insect living on a rock moving around the sun, and did his birth and death mean nothing in the history of the universe? Even if the world substance was immanent in him and he a particular mode of its activities, what good did it do him when he was not a master of his own destiny?

Boris returned the book to Berman and related his reactions to Spinoza's philosophy.

"Don't be discouraged," said Berman, "There is much truth in Spinoza's ideas, but it is not the whole truth. Nobody can give us that, anyway. Science has developed greatly since Spinoza's time, and our notions of God change with our knowledge. But I believe that many men of science can accept the God of Spinoza."

"I can't understand that there can be educated people who still believe in the old-fashioned God. I understand that preachers have studied at colleges of high standing and must have learned something about modern science, and still they read the old childish stories to their congregations. I have learned that even some prominent scientists believe in the God of the Bible. How is this possible?"

"Religion has many aspects," said Berman. "For many it is a tradition, learned in childhood and immutable like many ingrown habits of thought. For others it is a code of conduct, an ethical code, without which brutality would be the highest virtue, and the only law would be that of the jungle. Others regard it as an expression for the value and dignity of the individual and of his soul, which they firmly believe to be immortal. Many regard religion as a communion with a Supreme Being or a Universal Power, who loves man and cares for each individual. Many never speak about God, but speak instead of Nature and its wonders, without inquiring about the origin and causes of the observed phenomena. Some claim that the idea of a God behind and above nature is a superstition which should be eliminated as soon as possible from modern thinking."

"I think I belong to the last category," said Boris,

"but I would like to study the problem from different angles. I have always tried to look beyond the world of phenomena. My teachers have told me that there is nothing to look for, but I want to be sure about that before I give up the search. But I certainly do not want to read any old stuff about miracles and saints. Those stories could fool our forefathers, but not me. Neither do I want to listen to spiritualists with their spooks and seances. I want to stand on solid ground, where we start from established knowledge and search for the truth, irrespective of whether the truth is pleasant or not."

Berman admired the young man's frankness. He understood well the critical and somewhat suspicious and even arrogant attitude of this son of the modern era, the era inaugurated by Galileo and Newton, which had given us tools, airplanes and radio and had revealed a strange world in distant stars, in the atoms around us, and in the cells of our bodies.

"I think I can help you," said Berman. "Some days ago I spoke to a friend of mine, a retired professor of philosophy by the name of Albert Wilson, about organizing a little group to discuss the problems you have in mind. He is an idealist and a kind old gentleman, and I have no doubt that he will be glad to bring together some people of quite different opinions and let them fight it out. There is a physicist named Thomas Nelson who claims the world is a machine and loves to argue with the professor about it. I think you would enjoy listening to the clash of the swords in the battle of conflicting ideas. It is a free-for-all fight, and you may like to join it."

"I would like to," Boris said, "but I know nothing about philosophy. Even the scientific part may be too deep for me."

"Do not worry about that. We shall speak a language all of us can understand, and anybody who does not understand the details can freely ask for an explanation. It is all very informal."

"That's grand," said Boris. "Call me up when the first meeting has been arranged. Here is my telephone number."

"Take your violin with you!" said Berman.

"O.K.," said Boris, who had picked up some American slang.

CHAPTER 2

A World of Things and a World of Shadows

"I STILL CLAIM that the sun I see is in my mind and not somewhere in the sky," said Paul Berman at the first meeting of "The Searchers."

Thomas Nelson's face became a crimson red and he had difficulty in restraining himself. He said only, "I suppose you do not believe there is a sun at all and you think the astronomers are talking nonsense when they say that the sun has a surface temperature of six thousand degrees centigrade, and is at a distance of about ninety million miles. Have you not noticed that it gets warmer when the sun is shining? What is it then that produces this heat? I am a skeptic myself but, when I see something and can corroborate my observations in many ways, I do not doubt my senses."

The meeting of "The Searchers" took place in the home of Albert Wilson, a retired Professor of Philosophy. He was a kind old gentleman, slightly bent and with piercing, gray eyes. He was an idealist and an optimist, somewhat old-fashioned in his ideas, but well-informed about the new developments in many fields of research. Paul Berman, who made the startling remark about the sun being in his mind, was a Jewish physician and psychologist, well-read in philosophy, and he loved to startle his friends with paradoxical statements. Thomas Nelson, who answered Berman, was a teacher in physics, a matter-of-fact man who knew his field and hated mysticism, which he called obscurantism.

Wilson used to say that Nelson was an incorrigible realist, and when Nelson, not knowing exactly if this was flattering or not, asked what he meant by that, he said that a realist was a man who believed that the world was what it looked like. Nelson retorted that he would rather be a realist than a metaphysician who, in his opinion, was a philosopher of an almost extinct breed, who talked about things he knew nothing about. He said that philosophers claimed that metaphysics was the "science of the real" but, so far as he could see, it was an unscientific study of "things that weren't there."

Among the other members of the group present at the meeting was Edwin Willard, a mechanical engineer of wide experience, our friend Boris Charkoff, a Russian-born immigrant of the intellectual type and a gifted musician. Present was also Dr. John Davis, a minister who was too advanced in his teaching to suit fully the congregation in which he preached. He was a man of high character and a great friend of Wilson's.

Berman smiled a little at Nelson's remark. He was quite pleased with it, since it was just what he had been waiting for, and he was well-prepared for an answer. "I did not say that there was not beyond ourselves something we may call the sun and which gives us heat. I said simply that the sun I *see* is in my mind. Nobody has ever seen the sun of which you are talking. There is one picture of it in your mind and another in my mind, and in our minds we therefore picture it as being beyond both of us. But if we combine two mental pictures, we get nothing but a new mental picture."

"I suppose you believe that there are two suns, one in your vision and one far out in space," said Nelson. "I have no objection to that, but I would say that, by studying the sun in our vision, we can find out about the sun in space. So after all it is the external sun we study in a telescope or a spectroscope. Then there is no need to talk about an inner sun and an outer sun, since they are both the same thing."

"I do not believe at all that they are the same thing," said Berman. "There is about the same difference between them as between a man and his photograph, or between a man and his shadow. I might learn something about a man by studying his shadow, but I would learn very little that way. I might use a microscope to study the cells in his body and I would learn more by this method, but I still would be studying shadows of a man and not the man himself."

Edwin Willard, the engineer, had been listening carefully. Evidently something was brewing in his mind and he was eager to take part in the discussion. Polite as he was, he had waited for a lull in the proceedings. Now he jumped in with a broadside.

"When I build a bridge, I don't care a bit for its shadow or its picture. I am interested in the strength of the material, the load to which it is to be submitted, the cost of material and labor, and the profit to the builders and to myself. When I refer to the bridge I mean the real thing and not a phantom in my mind."

Berman was taken off guard by this reference to practical engineering. Wilson noticed his friend Berman's hesitation and wanted to give him time for an adequate answer. So he asked Willard the following question: "In your opinion, what is a bridge?"

"We all know what a bridge is," Willard said. "It is used to facilitate transportation. A strong bridge is made of steel and should stand on reinforced concrete."

"Do you know what steel is?" Wilson asked.

"Sure I do. It is iron combined with some carbon to give it proper strength. Iron and carbon are chemical elements with well-known properties. I feel that you are driving at something, but I do not quite see what it is."

The old man smiled a little and said, "When you

A World of Things and Shadows

speak about the properties of the chemical elements you must mean a particular type of knowledge acquired by a being with certain sense organs and mental idiosyncrasies. What sense organs do the scientists use when they study the physical and chemical properties of matter?"

Berman suddenly jerked his head back and his eyes began to shine. He realized the purpose of the professor's strange questioning of Willard. But he said nothing.

Willard was a little surprised at the question, but answered without any hesitation. "I think we use all our sense organs when we study matter. But the properties of matter are derived by indirect methods, and particularly by measurements. The data we find are co-ordinated into a consistent system of thought. Then we develop theories and bring order into the observed phenomena. And then we apply our knowledge to the making of a good bridge."

The eager Berman now jumped into the discussion and asked Willard, "Do you put your nose to your bridge to find out how it smells? Or do you touch it with your tongue to ascertain if it has any taste? Or do you listen to the dance of the electrons in the steel? Or do you touch it to find out if the steel is strong enough? Or does the color of the paint tell you whether it is a good bridge or not? Certainly you do not use all your sense organs when you study a bridge."

"You know well that these are not the methods we use," Willard said with a smile. "The hardness of steel can be determined by letting a ball of certain weight fall from a certain height on a polished steel plate and measuring the diameter of the depression. The weight of steel is determined on a balance, and its strength by stretching it by a measured force. The structure of steel can be studied by x-rays, and even by an electron microscope, which shows many details which an optical microscope cannot reveal. Nelson can corroborate the statement that an atom of iron has a nucleus fifty-six times as heavy as that of the hydrogen atom, and has twenty-six electrons outside the nucleus, which itself has a positive electric charge equal to that of the twenty-six electrons. We know how iron behaves under different conditions, and that is all we engineers need to know."

"This is all very interesting," said Berman, "but does it not strike you that all these properties refer to the structure of iron and to qualities dependent upon its structure? When you describe a structure you use measurements of length and relative position of points which in some way are characteristic for the substance. After all, you are only talking about structures with space and time properties which, in principle at least, you can see with your eyes. The number of electrons in an atom of iron is a characteristic of a structure, not of iron, but of a model of an atom created by the men of science. The whole science of physics seems to be

A World of Things and Shadows

based on measurements of space and time intervals and structural properties. When you study an x-ray photograph of a film of steel, you are studying the shadow of steel and not steel itself. When you study an atom, you are indirectly studying the structure of a shadow in your mind. Physics is a study of a play of shadows, but the substance which produces the shadow is completely unknown to you. So, after all, it is the shadow of a bridge that you are talking about, and not the bridge itself."

There was silence in the room, after this harangue. Nelson felt that he should object to this strange outburst, but he did not immediately know how best to answer the preposterous statements. Wilson beamed, but said nothing. It was Boris Charkoff who made the first remark.

"Dr. Berman, if you were a soldier in a war and saw a tank coming towards you with blazing guns, you would probably think that the tank was a moving shadow in your mind, and that it was made of the same stuff that dreams are made of. You could see no reason to dodge it and something would soon hit you, but you probably would never know or care what it was."

"I am pretty sure I would dodge the tank," said Berman. "I have dodged cars in my dreams; it may be a habit, but it is a very good habit. Once I was hit by a car in my dream and I felt quite a pain, and the excitement forced the blood to my brain, and I woke up. I have even heard of a man who was permanently injured in an automobile accident in a dream. It was probably autosuggestion, but therefore not less effective.

"Sincerely speaking, I do not deny that a tank, a bridge, or the sun may be quite real, that is, they have an existence independent of my mind. But my knowledge of them is entirely dependent on what type of mind I have. Therefore, in describing them I am also describing the type of mind with which I was born and the present stage of the science of physics. If I had been born with sense organs and a mental equipment quite different from those of other men, I am certain that my description of the sun and of matter would be almost unintelligible to other human beings; although there may be a few elements, like numbers, for instance, which I might share with ordinary men."

Wilson had been listening with great attention and now joined the discussion. "Eddington claims that all our knowledge of the physical world could have been reached by visual sensation alone, or rather from colorless sensations of changing structures. The constants of physics according to him can all be derived from the fact that physical space has three dimensions and time has only one. Whether he is correct or not, I shall leave to the theoretical physicists to find out. I think Berman is right when he says that physics starts from shadows and therefore never reaches the substance. Nobody knows what an electron is, but only how it acts. Some people claim that the problem 'what

A World of Things and Shadows

matter is' is a nonsensical question, and 'how it acts' is the only question which we can answer. But at any event, we must realize that our knowledge of matter is limited to certain aspects, conditioned by our sense organs and our type of mind."

Nelson did not like this pronouncement of the venerable professor to go entirely unchallenged. He said, "Why should we try to go beyond our immediate experience into a world which may well be beyond our reach and understanding? We can learn enough about matter to use it for making good bridges, automobiles and airplanes. If we had peace in the world, everybody could have food and comfort and could enjoy life. Can we really expect more of life than that? I do not want to be mystified by any religious cult or pseudo-science, which may only draw people's attention from the realities of life. I do not want to waste my time chasing a pot of imaginary gold at the foot of a rainbow."

Wilson thought a little and said: "If we look carefully, we may find more valuable things than gold hidden behind the phenomena we observe. Man, like the higher animals, has an instinct to maintain his life and may even fight for his survival. He differs from animals, however, in that he has a desire to acquire knowledge for its own sake, feeling that knowledge and truth have a value of their own, a value which ignorance and untruth can never have. Being intelligent beings, we want to find out for ourselves where we are going and to be able to set a course towards the most sublime goal we can imagine. Of course, there are people who, like cattle, want to be led to the feed boxes, and who have no desire to do their own thinking."

"That is all very well," said Nelson, "and I may agree with you that knowledge may have a value beyond that pertaining to its useful applications. A mathematician may be fascinated by a new discovery in the relationship of mathematical functions, even if his discovery seemingly is of no earthly use. I think he feels that he is looking at a realm with a beautiful logical consistency, and that he has found something of value belonging to a world beyond that revealed by our sense organs. I doubt, however, that a study of matter can tell us anything about the meaning of human life and about the goal to which mankind is striving. And above all, can it make us happy?"

When Nelson spoke about happiness and life, Dr. Davis, the clergyman, felt that he should say something. Looking out into space he said:

"Children and savages can be happy without knowing anything about the secrets of life and of the universe. Temporarily it is good for us to become like little children and enjoy every minute of our activity. But carried too far it prevents us from developing our mental faculties. This development always involves effort, and in most cases also pain and sorrow, but the happiness we derive from this development is of a higher order than that of a child or a playing puppy. I think it even indicates the meaning of the human life. Jesus of Nazareth said that the truth shall make us free. People may have quite different opinions about what the truth is, but everybody admits that science has found some truth that was unknown to our ancestors of a few centuries back."

While listening to Davis' pronouncement Wilson went to his bookcase in search for a book which he soon found. After looking at the very last sentence in the book he said to Nelson:

"Do you think Max Planck is a mystic?"

"Certainly not," said Nelson. "He is the man who discovered the quantum of action, and he is regarded as one of the founders of modern physics."

"This statement by Planck may surprise you," said Wilson. "It is the concluding remark in his book 'The Universe in the Light of Modern Physics.' He writes: 'Modern physics impresses us particularly with the truth of the old doctrine which teaches that there are realities existing apart from our sense-perceptions, and that there are problems and conflicts where these realities are of a greater value for us than the richest treasures of the world of experience.' Evidently Planck had in mind the rules recently found to govern the elementary processes in physics, and he regards these rules as symbols of a world beyond that of our direct perception and more real than the world of sense phenomena."

"I am a little surprised at this statement by Planck," said Nelson, "in particular about his apparent contention that these so-called realities are of much greater value for us than the world of our experience. I would say that their value lies entirely in the fact that they can help us to understand how nature works, and then we can apply our new knowledge, as we have recently done in the liberation of atomic energy."

As was to be expected Willard, the practical engineer, expressed his full agreement with Nelson, the realistic physicist.

"Interpretation of nature," he said, "is a help in science and engineering, but should not be regarded as indicative of any ultimate realities, as the metaphysicians claim."

Boris nodded his consent to the opinions expressed by the practical men, but could not think of anything pertinent to add to their statements.

Berman could barely keep silent during this attack on philosophy in general and metaphysics in particular. In an excited voice he said:

"Suppose you were studying a living cell and saw strange motions going on in the cytoplasm. I suppose a practical man would look for a mechanism responsible for the motions and be satisfied when he had found a complete chain of physical and chemical processes which, in his opinion, could explain everything. He would be like an intelligent ant studying a running watch. He would notice that one wheel was driven

A World of Things and Shadows

by another, and he might insert a grain of sand which would stop the clock, or even remove a wheel to speed up the clock. But if the ant were less of an engineer and more of a philosopher and a metaphysician, he would ask himself, who has made this intricate mechanism, what keeps it going, why does it stop, and what is the purpose of the watch? He might not get very far in his search for truth, but he realizes at least that there is a mystery, and he feels an urge to solve it. He may find several facts about mechanics and about the properties of matter, and who can tell whether in the end he may not find some secrets of life which may make him the master of his own fate. There, I think, lies the great hidden treasure of realities of which Planck speaks."

There was a long silence after Berman's impassioned speech. After a while Wilson remarked:

"I think we all need time to consider the points raised, and I hope we shall in future meetings have many opportunities to discuss them further. For the present I want only to add that the very fact that there is something we call matter in the universe, that there are rules for its activities, and that there are intelligent beings who can study matter, derive the rules, and ponder over them, are important data in the world of our experience.

"Perhaps Mr. Charkoff will play something for us on the violin while we are having a cup of tea. It will be ready in a few minutes."

Boris played some classical music. The sound of Schumann's *Traumerei* vibrated through the room. Nothing was said while the soft music reached into unknown depths of the souls of the listeners.

When Boris stopped, Nelson suddenly remarked: "I can see that there is one thing that does not belong to the world of physics. That is the music we have just heard."

"Only God can make music like that," said Davis.

"Shucks!" said Boris, "It was I who made the sound."

"I am sure you did not make any sound at all," Wilson said. "You simply set the strings in vibration in a certain way and for a definite purpose. The vibrations in the air affected our ears, and certain nerve cells were stimulated, and this opened the gates between our consciousness and another world, of which we would have no knowledge if we did not have these nerve cells.

"But thanks for the music. It was grand!"

CHAPTER 3

Gravitation

"AT OUR last meeting," said Dr. Wilson, "we spoke about matter, and I think we agreed that, due to the specific properties of our sense organs and our mind, our knowledge of the intrinsic properties of matter is limited to its structural properties. In studying matter we are actually studying a play of shadows in our consciousness. But we can use matter to our own advantage; some kind of matter is needed as food and clothing, other kinds can be used to build bridges and automobiles. Among other things we said that the sun we actually see is in our mind, and from the visual picture of the sun which we observe with our eyes or aided by instruments of different kinds we can construct a scientific picture of the sun, a picture, however, which, because we are human beings with specific kinds of sense organs and with a particular type of imagery, is limited to certain aspects. We concluded that the sun, like matter in general, is not only a play of shadows in our mind, but behind the observed shadow play we suspected the existence of something which could not be described in physical terms, that is, as structures.

"This evening we shall discuss a type of phenomena, so common that few people ever think about them. We are going to discuss the problems connected with gravity, a subject which I know is of great interest to some of you. To start the discussion I shall propound a question. What is gravity? Let us first hear what a practical engineer has to say, and I call on Willard to answer this question from his standpoint."

"I would say that gravity is an idea we have of the cause of bodies having weight. It takes a large muscular effort to lift a big stone and a smaller effort to lift a little one, and the big stone presses harder against the ground than does the little one. The cause of such phenomena we call gravity. It acts like a force directed downward, that is, towards the center of the earth. It causes a body which can move freely to fall downward at an accelerated speed, and the increase in velocity at the earth's surface is the same for all bodies and is about thirty-two feet per second for every second it travels, provided that the fall is not impeded in any way, as it is in the air. The force of gravity extends to all material bodies, and Newton has shown that it is proportional to the masses of the attracting bodies and decreases with the square of their mutual distances. I understand that this law has been modified by Einstein, but for moderate velocities Newton's law is accurate enough. Mechanical models based on motions or strains in an ether have been suggested to explain gravitational forces. I wish a satisfactory mechanism of gravity could be developed, but it seems that physicists nowadays look with disfavor on any mechanical interpretation of gravity. They appear to be satisfied when they know how gravity acts and shun the problem of its inherent nature or cause, a problem which they claim to be outside the science of physics."

Wilson thanked Willard for his excellent description of gravity. "Your statement that gravity is an idea of the cause of something observable appeals to me personally. In order to understand gravity we must first learn how it acts, and I suggest that we first talk about this subject. I suppose Nelson has something to say about it."

"Yes, I have," said Nelson. "But first I want to express my satisfaction with Willard's description of the way gravity works. I agree with the scientists who can see no reason to try to penetrate into its more fundamental nature, if it has any, and who are satisfied with a quantitative formulation. Much nonsense could be avoided if people stuck to facts and avoided speculation. An interesting feature of gravity is that it is not affected by any physical or chemical transformations. It is this aspect of gravity which makes the balance such a useful tool in chemistry, which

Lavoisier was the first to recognize. Willard's characterization of gravity as the cause of bodies having weight is, I think, not the best definition, and I would say that its property of affecting the motions of bodies is more fundamental. Gravity depends upon our motion, and the weight of bodies may therefore be quite different for different observers.

"For example, when an elevator starts moving upwards, every object in the elevator presses against the bottom, and apparently all objects in the elevator are heavier than when the elevator is stationary. The increase in weight can be measured by a spring balance, and we find that all bodies have acquired an increase in weight proportional to their normal weight and to the change in speed of the elevator. When the elevator starts moving down, all the bodies become lighter. If the sustaining cable should break, the elevator would fall down freely. From the very moment when the free fall started, all effects of gravity would have disappeared, although the people in the elevator probably would be too excited to notice it. We can well realize that they are falling at the same rate as the elevator itself, and the people and the objects in the elevator no longer press against its bottom. In the same way, if we imagine a group of people in a space ship, coasting along in space like a planet, they could not detect any effect of gravity by the usual kinds of measurements performed within the ship. Similarly, if people could live on a little asteroid they would have no

Gravitation

appreciable weight and, if they jumped ever so little, they would be in danger of leaving their abode, never to return. By them, gravity would certainly not be described as the cause of bodies having weight. Rather they would describe gravity as the cause of the curvature in the orbit of their ship."

"I understand that a uniform motion has no influence on gravity," said Wilson.

"According to the theory of relativity a uniform motion has no effect on gravity or on anything else," was Nelson's retort. "This seems to be well established by experiments. All physical constants, including the velocity of light, are the same for two observers moving with uniform velocity relative to one another. I should add that the people in a space ship, even if they never saw the sun, the stars, or the planets, need not be ignorant of gravity, in spite of the fact that their bodies had no weight, and they could hover freely in midair. With sensitive instruments they could measure a very small attraction between bodies close together."

"It seems to me that we are using the word force with two different meanings," Berman then remarked. "On the one hand we mean something similar to a muscular tension, and it is measured by the elongation of a spring or a rubber band. We also use the term as the imagined cause of a deviation from a uniform motion, and we then measure it as an acceleration multiplied by a factor called mass, which is proportional to the weight as measured at the earth's surface. Which of these two definitions is the most fundamental?"

Nelson was quick to answer the physician. "Primitive people, who are not concerned with theories of the motion of bodies on the earth or in the sky, would naturally think of a force in terms of muscular efforts and of tensions and would measure it with instruments like spring balances. It is for this reason that, up to the time of Galileo, force was associated with the notion of tension or muscular efforts. Galileo's definition of a force as the product of mass and acceleration is the more fundamental and is applicable everywhere and is of great importance in the computation of the effects of gravitation and other forces. Lately the term force has been replaced by purely geometrical concepts, but I cannot see any particular advantage in it."

"There is something here I do not quite understand," said Berman. "Here is a book resting on this table. The book presses down on the table and the table presses upwards on the book. The two forces must be equal since the book does not move either down or up. The book has no acceleration, consequently according to Galileo's definition of force as a product of mass and acceleration, there is no force acting on it. But certainly there is a gravitational force pressing it against the table, and the two definitions of force seem to be contradictory. Even if two opposite forces are in complete balance and there is no resultant motion, there is still a strain left, which would not be there if no forces were acting."

Nelson replied again. "When Galileo propounded his definition of a force he had in mind a body freely moving under the influence of gravity. Obviously if I throw a stone and it hits something it is no longer influenced by gravity alone, but by another body or bodies. A stone resting on the ground tends to move down with a definite acceleration, but its motion is prevented by the ground. It is just this restraint in its free fall that is the cause of the pressure, and therefore the two ways of measuring forces are equivalent. A drunkard, who tells you that the reason his walk is wobbly is that the ground moves up and hits him all the time, has a remarkably clear notion of gravity, although his thinking otherwise may be rather confused. The reason why I feel that my body presses against the ground is due to the fact that the earth prevents me from falling down. We may say that it is the molecules in the earth's surface pressing against my feet, which I describe as a gravitational force or pressure. Weight and pressure and tensions are Nature's opposition to freedom of motion."

Wilson remarked, thoughtfully, "If we want to study gravity in its purest form, I suppose that we have to imagine ourselves in a space ship. When the ship is propelled upwards from the earth, I am convinced that we would feel a tremendous increase in gravity. As soon as there is no longer any force propelling the ship and when we move in a vacuum, practically all effects of gravity will disappear. This is contrary to Jules Verne's description of a journey to the moon. I think Jules Verne was wrong when he thought that gravity would disappear only at a certain place between the earth and the moon."

"Yes, Jules Verne was wrong," said Nelson. "Nobody has yet tried any journey in a space ship but I have no doubt that it will be done in the future. We know quite well how gravity would act inside the ship. I do not think, however, that we could learn much about gravity in a space ship without looking at other objects or studying their motion, because gravitational forces would be extremely small. But we could study inertia which is closely related to gravity. In fact, we may well regard inertia and gravity as different aspects of the same natural phenomenon. In the space ship we would find that a big body would be difficult to set in motion and difficult to stop. We would not call a big body heavy, but we might call it massive, and we could measure the degree of massiveness by letting bodies collide. This would be a determination of the masses of weightless bodies. Since the weight of a body is something specific to our abode, the earth, and varies from one planet to another, it must be replaced by mass in all scientific investigations."

"We ordinarily think of mass as being a measure of the inertia of a body," Wilson said, "but evidently we

Gravitation

have to use the same mass when we describe gravitational effects at a particular place. I understand that the equality of mass as determined by collisions and by weighing, respectively, is one of the cornerstones in Einstein's general theory of relativity. I suppose that many people regard matter as the cause of gravity. Therefore, if there were no matter in the universe, or rather just enough to supply us with some test bodies, the motions of which we could study, there would be no gravity. Since mass and gravity are intimately connected, we may well assume that in this case bodies would have no mass. If there were no stars and nebulae far out in space, there would be almost no inertia, little energy would be needed to set our automobiles in motion or to stop them, and when they collided no damage would be done. Is this hypothesis in accordance with modern physics?"

Nelson nodded. "I think it is. But it is not necessary to regard the matter in the star systems as the actual cause of inertia, since we cannot annihilate matter and study the consequences. Our concept of cause implies something previous in time to its effects. It would obviously be impossible to prove that matter came first, and then came inertia as the result."

Wilson continued. "If we admit a close relationship, even if it is not a causal one, between the amount of matter in the universe and the weight of a body on the earth, we should be able to figure out how much matter there is in the whole universe. Eddington has figured out that the mass of all the matter in the universe is equivalent to 10^{76} hydrogen atoms. I do not know what weight we can attach to this statement, but it seems to be a fact that this number, whatever it may signify, can be derived from our physical constants."

"I do not know what this large number really means, and the experts have been rather noncommittal about it," Nelson said. "But nowadays we have no objection to a universe of finite size and containing a finite amount of matter. Formerly it was thought that space must extend indefinitely in all directions, since one could not conceive of a boundary beyond which there was no space at all. But a finite space need not have any boundary. The earth has a finite surface, yet no matter how far we may travel we never reach a boundary, and all points on the surface are equivalent. If we send a beam of light out into space, it does not necessarily go farther and farther out, because the matter in the universe bends the beam around, and after a very long time it may pass near the region from where it started. It may, of course, be scattered, absorbed and re-emitted, but like a traveler on the earth's surface, it can never leave a finite universe. In fact, a finite universe is easier to understand than an infinite universe, in which the radiation is forever lost in a bottomless abyss. In a finite universe there is no center and no boundary, all parts are equivalent, just as on the earth's surface."

Gravitation

"I have talked with people," Willard said, "who have no difficulty in understanding that there can be mutual attraction between bodies, but they can not understand the idea of a *gravitational field*. They think of gravitational forces as similar to those produced by stretched springs or rubber bands joining all the bodies in the universe. I have tried to explain that around every body and therefore in any system of bodies we may imagine a condition of some sort that causes a particle of matter to become accelerated in a definite direction and by a definite amount. When these accelerations are plotted, they constitute a continuous set of lines of force completely defined in any part of space, and these lines of force exist even in the absence of any particles. If the particles are small enough, they can be regarded as test bodies or indicators which themselves have no appreciable effect on the field. But when they then ask how a body can act where it is not, I have to admit that I do not know."

Nelson explained. "There is a definition of force other than those we have considered, which is more directly connected with the concept of force fields. We can define a force in any particular direction as the change in energy per unit length in the given direction. It takes no force to keep a body moving along a horizontal surface in the absence of friction and air resistance. The earth exerts no force along a horizontal surface because this is a surface of constant energy, but it takes a definite amount of energy to raise a body of a given weight one foot, and this change in energy is manifested as a force. This way of expressing force leads directly to the law of conservation of energy."

Berman, the logician, remarked, "It seems to me that this definition of force is no definition at all. If we define energy as a product of a force and a length, we cannot later define force as an energy difference per unit length."

"Your objection would be entirely justified if we always measured energy in terms of forces," Nelson explained. "Uniform motion is a form of energy, but we should not associate it with any forces. We have all reasons to believe that energy is more fundamental than force, and in defining force we should base it on something more fundamental than itself."

Wilson smiled a little at this remark by the matter-of-fact physicist and said, "I am very glad to see that our friend Nelson is looking for realities behind the world of our experience and therefore has become a metaphysician, but I doubt very much that he will admit being afflicted by their dreadful mental disease. I think he is right in regarding forces as the manifestations of energy differences. I like to picture a gravitational field around the earth as a series of concentric spherical shells representing surfaces of constant gravitational energy. We have difficulties in picturing forces which do not act on anything, but we have learned to picture energy in a potential form, an energy that is not doing anything observable, but is

Gravitation 39

capable of doing mechanical work under the right conditions. The force of gravity seems to represent, in amount as well as in direction, the tendency of a body to move to a level of less energy.

"Nelson said that mass was something intrinsic in matter and that it was not changed by any physical or chemical transformations. But according to the theory of relativity the mass of a body is a function of its motion. We can thus change the mass of a body by setting it in rapid motion. Since all velocities are primarily referred to an observer's framework in space and time and only indirectly to other bodies, it seems to me that the increase in mass expresses primarily a relationship between an external object and the observer's mental framework in space and time."

"I object to the statement that motion in general and an increase in mass in particular have anything to do with the mind," Nelson said. "They would occur even if there were no living beings on the earth who could describe them. I must admit, however, that it is not easy to give a simple reason for this increase in mass. I can understand that we cannot indefinitely increase the speed of an electrically charged body, like an electron, since an electric field cannot travel faster than light, but why we cannot indefinitely increase the speed of a body that has no electric charge is more difficult to understand."

"I think it moves in your mind and not in an external space," said Wilson. "Motion is the human way of expressing certain changes in the external world, but it is not the only way and it is probably not the way that comes nearest the truth. In space-time there is no real motion, yet it expresses the nature of what we call motion in the most perfect way."

Boris Charkoff had been listening attentively to the arguments. He had heard similar discussions at the university, and his professor had explained everything by writing down some complex equations involving what he called tensors, but he had never really understood the meaning of the strange symbols with many subscripts and superscripts. With the unsophisticated directness of youth he asked:

"Why is it that we cannot move a heavy body in any way we wish without any effort at all? And if we have set a heavy body in motion, why can we not stop it without muscular effort? If we admit that nature determines how a body with a given initial velocity shall move in a given gravitational field, it is still not clear to me by what method it opposes my effort to move it along another path or at a speed different from that imposed by nature. It seems that mass is the *measure* of nature's opposition to our interference with its normal activities, but not the actual *cause* of the opposition."

Nelson felt that this was a challenge to him, and he replied. "In the first place I want to repeat that science is a description in quantitative terms of the way nature works, and it does not pretend to explain how

Gravitation

these effects are brought about. Further, when we interfere with the natural path of a moving body, we do it by interposing additional fields, like the field in an obstruction or in our muscles. We describe such fields as structures in space and time, because our description is derived from effects and not from causes of which we know nothing, and any discussion of them is useless."

"I do not think it is useless to discuss anything," Berman remarked, "because in discussing our problems we are forced to think about them, and nobody can tell beforehand if something of great importance may not turn up as the result of our discussions and cogitation. The first thing that has come to my mind as a result of this discussion is that mass seems to be a measure of the strength of the ties that bind a body to the rest of the matter in the universe. Since all atomic nuclei have weights which very nearly are integral multiples of the weight of the nucleus of the hydrogen atom, we may perhaps regard the mass of an atom as representing its number of ties to the universe, or rather to a frame defined statistically by all the stars in the whole universe.

"Further, in answer to Nelson's assertion that we do not know anything about the causes of force fields, I want to state that there is one particular case in which we have direct knowledge of the cause of changes in a field of force. I am talking about the changes in the shape of our muscles that can be controlled by our will. In this case the primary cause is not an interference of many fields, but something in my conscious mind that causes contractions in my muscles. Will seems to be a mode of my mind that can guide physical movements in a predetermined direction, as when I write a meaningful sentence. I know there are scientists who claim that my will is a feeling resulting from chemical changes in my brain caused by my writing the sentence, but I think that only very few men seriously believe in this theory. I am no automaton and I know that my will precedes my writing and does not follow it."

When Berman mentioned the word mode Boris' eyes began to shine. Had he not recently read Spinoza's *Ethics* where this excommunicated Dutch Jew spoke about a world substance with different modes of action. Perhaps gravity and inertia were such modes of this profound substance, which was supposed to be the ultimate cause of everything, including the orderly processes in nature. Spinoza spoke about a *natura naturans*, the active substance, and a *natura naturata*, the results of its activities. He also spoke about the necessity of looking at nature "sub specie eternitatis," from the aspect of eternity, which Boris interpreted as meaning that we should look at nature from the point of view of an eternal world order. Spinoza identified the world substance with a God, but his God was quite different from that of the ignorant crowd. A world substance behind nature and manifested as physical phenomena? Perhaps there really was something in that! A friendly smile from Berman gave him courage when he said:

"Is it not possible that, as Spinoza claims, behind all phenomena in nature there is a substance that governs everything and appears in different modes? One of its modes of action we observe as gravitational fields with definite properties in space and time. If it is responsible for all space-time structures, it is also responsible for those changes in the muscles of my hand which are acting in the writing of a sentence."

An expression of disgust appeared on Nelson's face when he said, "I hope you do not mean that you believe that there is a God who decides how fast a body shall fall, and how much effort is needed to set an automobile in motion, or what is written in the newspapers. Is that what they teach in Russia?"

Boris was well aware of the sarcasm in Nelson's outburst and answered somewhat heatedly. "We certainly do not teach that in Russia. We are a practical people and nearly all of us have things to do of more immediate importance than a search for the realities behind the world of phenomena. But when the time comes when we no longer have to work so hard for our livelihood and for our comfort, we may develop a philosophy of our own. It will be a philosophy, or call it a religion if you like, based on science and on facts, and not on any alleged revelations. If we want a God, it will be a God as revealed by nature and described by science. We shall find out about God in our laboratories and not in any musty documents. And our best scientists will be our high priests, who tell us what is true and not true."

Davis thought it was high time for him to take down science from the high pedestal on which Boris had placed it. "There are things greater than knowledge," he said. "What good does it do us if we know the secrets of the atoms if we only use them for destruction and to promote our self-interest and lust for power? Goodness is more important than knowledge. I would rather live in a world of good men, than in a world of learned men. A learned man is not necessarily a wise man, but a good man is wise in his goodness, even if he be ignorant in many ways. Christ was not a learned man, but he was a good man and a wise man.

"I am not defending Christianity as it is preached and practiced by most people today. But the fundamental laws of Christianity are to love God and to love thy neighbor as thyself. The love of God means a love of those principles which our conscience tells us are good and helpful for all, irrespective of nationality, race, creed, or color. It is accompanied by an admiration of His wisdom and a desire to come in close contact with the source of all life and of our own mind, so that we can live in harmony with His principles. I do not think the God of Spinoza differs so much from that of the Christians, the Mohammedans, the Budhists, or the God of the old Chinese. God is the personification of the principles that govern the universe, and His main attribute is Love. Even a young child or an ignorant savage can understand that kind of a god."

Boris was rather puzzled by this pronouncement by the old clergyman. He felt instinctively that something of importance had been said, although he had never deliberately given it any thought. His whole training had been devoted to the learning of scientific facts and to their application in engineering. Love and goodness had no place in the edifice of science, as he had envisaged it, but they certainly were important factors in the life of the individual and in human relationship. He had heard Soviet scientists claim that motherly love was a biological reaction that could be induced in a female animal by inoculation with prolactin, a hormone that, if he remembered rightly, could be produced in the laboratory. Was that feeling of love in the prolactin itself? If it were not in the prolactin, where did it come from? Where do our feelings and emotions really come from? And colors and sounds?

Boris' thoughts were interrupted by the voice of Wilson.

"I think we had better discuss these problems at another time, when we can more thoroughly study them. They are very important, and we can not easily turn them aside."

CHAPTER 4

Expanding Waves and Small Particles

AT THE next meeting of "The Searchers" Boris was a little late. When he arrived at the home of Dr. Wilson, he saw his friends gathered around Berman, who was sitting in a chair at a table looking horizontally through an eye-piece. A few feet in front of the eye-piece was a lens covered by an opaque screen with two large holes, side by side. Berman was evidently looking at a lighted electric lamp in the corner of the room, the lamp being covered by a screen with a small hole, through which the light was shining. Boris asked Nelson, who seemed to be in charge of the demonstration, what it was all about. Nelson told him that they were studying the interference of light. When Boris' turn came to look into the eye-piece, he saw a bright image crossed by a number of dark lines. He had seen somewhat similar demonstrations of the interference of light, but he did not know what was the purpose of the present experiment. When they all had looked at the image in the eye-piece, they seated themselves in their comfortable chairs.

Wilson opened the meeting. "Tonight we shall discuss a problem that has been the subject of much discussion in recent years. I am referring to the important discovery that light, which for a century has been known to have the properties of a wave motion, also acts as if it consisted of small particles. Some years ago Sir William Bragg said in a lecture that on Mondays, Wednesdays, and Fridays light acted as waves, but on Tuesdays, Thursdays, and Saturdays it acted as particles. Since today is a Saturday we could expect light to act as particles, but in the arrangement our friend Nelson has set up, it seems to consist of waves.

"Since Bragg gave his lecture, the mystery has deepened. Some years ago it was found that electrons, which everybody believed to be particles, acted as waves in certain types of experiments. It has all been very confusing with this conflicting evidence, but I believe that from this conflict will come a deeper understanding of nature. Mathematical physicists have developed profound theories to explain the puzzle, theories which have forced us to scrutinize the very foundation of our knowledge as derived from physical measurements. It has been found that nature can still be regarded as rational, but it does not act in the way our childish notions, developed from our experience with gross bodies, think it should act. I have no doubt that we have just discovered and opened a hidden gate, and we see a path leading to a new domain in the field of human knowledge. I shall now ask Dr. Nelson to tell us something about the new discoveries concerning the nature of light."

Nelson started at once. "It has been known from time immemorial that light travels along straight paths. We all know that an object casts a shadow, and if the source of light is very small, the shadow has a sharp boundary and is of the same shape as that of a flat object placed perpendicular to the beam of light. It was therefore natural to assume that light consisted of very small particles, or corpuscles, as they are more properly called, a view to which Newton himself subscribed. But a closer inspection showed that the edges of a shadow were not as sharp as could be expected on such a theory. If a beam of parallel light is made to pass through a circular hole, the spot of light is of the same size as the hole itself. If we make the hole smaller, the spot of light also becomes smaller, but the edges become more diffused. If we make the hole smaller and smaller, we reach a stage when the spot clearly begins to *increase* in size, and when the hole is very small, the light spreads out in all directions, although, of course, it is very faint. The inevitable conclusion is that light does not always travel along straight lines, but is always bent at an edge. This is called the diffraction of light.

"The Dutch scientist Huygens suggested that light may be a wave motion in an elastic medium, called ether, and he could explain some of the observed phenomena on this assumption. For a time this wave theory of light was regarded as an alternative hypothesis, accepted by some scientists, but rejected by others. Fresnel, a young Frenchman, made a close study of the nature of light. At the beginning of the last century he presented a paper to the French Academy of Sciences in which he advocated the wave theory of light. A prominent Academician said at the discussion that it was preposterous to think of light as a wave motion, because then there must be a bright spot in the center of the shadow of a circular disk, if illuminated by a source of light on the axis of the disk. Fresnel immediately tried out the experiment, and to his great delight he found a bright spot in the center of the shadow. The discovery caused quite a sensation in the Academy. The corpuscular theory of light could not long survive this damaging blow and was soon discarded.

"The wave theory of light seemed at first to explain all known phenomena concerning light. The most startling application of the theory was perhaps the development of a method of producing spectra by letting light be reflected or transmitted by a surface with a great number of parallel lines, a so-called diffraction grating. But the corpuscular theory of light had an unexpected revival. In 1900 Planck discovered that the distribution of the frequencies of the light emitted by a hot body could only be explained on the assumption that the radiation emitted by an incandescent body consists of indivisible elements, the energy of each one of them being proportional to the frequency of the radiation. The factor of proportionality seemed to be a constant, which he called the Quantum of Action.

"It was later found that when ultra-violet light strikes certain metals, like sodium, the electrons emitted had a kinetic energy proportional, not to the intensity of the light as one might expect, but to its frequency, and that the factor of proportionality was again equal to the constant discovered by Planck. Apparently the elements of radiation can travel large distances without any loss of energy. Einstein then propounded a corpuscular theory of light, in which a light impulse was supposed to travel like an arrow from an emitting to an absorbing atom and carried a definite amount of energy in accordance with Planck's rule. The theory worked very well in explaining the transfer of energy from one atom to another at a great distance and without loss, but it left the well established wave nature of light totally unexplained.

"Let us now go back to the experiment which we performed at the beginning of our meeting. I had screened off all the light except that emitted by a short vertical section of the filament in the electric lamp in order to make the lateral width of the image of the light source so small that it did not obliterate the interference pattern. The light went through two holes in front of the lens, and the two beams, when meeting in the focal plane, produced bright and dark bands. The beam of light from one hole was evidently able to destroy the light from the other hole at certain places, while enhancing it at other places. This is the well-known phenomenon of interference of light. You all know the classical explanation in terms of an ether, in which a wave crest may fall on top of another and produce a strong wave, or a wave crest may fall on top of a trough, the crest and the trough annihilating one another. In the first case the light, which is supposed to be the result of the wave motion, is enhanced, and in the second case it is destroyed.

"There is a great mystery about the way light is propagated. The radiation appears to consist of small elements of energy, called photons, which disappear at one place and later reappear with unchanged characteristics at another place. The wave system of one photon cannot be added to that of another photon, a fact expressed by the statement that 'a photon can only interfere with itself.' We may say that a photon is completely isolated from other photons, similarly the wave system of one photon is completely isolated from that of another photon. A photon must be exceedingly small, since it can act on an individual atom and transmit its full energy to the absorbing atom. Nevertheless, its wave system must have a large extension, in particular when it has travelled from an atom in a distant star, when its wave system may sweep over the whole solar system. In our experiment the wave system of a photon must at least cover both the apertures to produce interference phenomena. How a greatly extended wave system can in an instant disappear except at one point, where its whole effect is concentrated, is very difficult to understand. You can now see why Bragg was so puzzled about the nature of light. The difficulty seems to lie in our inability to *picture* the true nature of light. Mathematically there is no great difficulty in predicting what will happen in any particular case, although our predictions are of a statistical nature only."

The leader of the group was evidently much pleased with his friend's exposition of the wave nature and particle nature of light. In thanking him he said again that he thought the difficulties were due to our propensity in picturing physical phenomena in terms familiar to our specific type of mind. He invited discussion, and Berman with his usual alertness began immediately.

"You said that light sometimes acts as particles and sometimes as waves, and I understand that it never acts as both at the same time. Can not a particle be guided by electromagnetic waves of the same type as

Expanding Waves and Small Particles   53

radio waves, and may it not be due to our ignorance that we cannot tell in which of the two beams the photon moves? If this is the case it may be possible to let the photon do something when it passes a hole without disturbing the coherence in the wave system."

"In ordinary light an individual photon carries only a very small amount of energy," Nelson replied, "although its effect can be detected and measured in the case of ultra-violet light, provided we use some amplifying device. The consensus of opinions among theoretical physicists seems to be that if a photon does anything observable at all, its state is changed in such a way that it can no longer interfere with other parts of the guiding beam. I think, however, the idea of guiding wave systems is an improper one. The question is not through which hole an individual photon moves, but rather whether it goes through one hole or through both, and all evidence indicates that it goes through both. How a small photon can go through both of the two holes in our experiment, I admit freely that I cannot explain."

"I think Nelson is correct in his statement that we must think of a photon going through both holes at the same time," Wilson remarked. "If we think of electromagnetic waves of the same type as those of radio waves as guiding photons in their motions, the energy of the beam can be expected to be partly in the waves and partly in the photons. But we know that the full energy is contained in the photons, and nothing is left to be carried by the electromagnetic waves. When a photon is absorbed, the whole wave system disappears instantaneously, however large it may be. I doubt greatly that there are any moving photons at all. Physicists lately have tried to get rid of unobservable elements, and it seems to me that a photon in transit is definitely an unobservable thing. Why not try to eliminate the moving photons and reserve them for cases when something actually happens?"

Berman, the metaphysician was immediately ready to elaborate on this idea of his old friend. "Perhaps you remember that at our first meeting I said that the world of which we have any immediate knowledge is in our own mind. To most of you, I am sure, this was a preposterous statement, for do we not see what happens in the external world, and do not other people see the same things as we see and see them in the same way? This argument is not conclusive, because we have all inherited the same type of mind and the same kind of sense organs, and our individual interpretations of nature therefore all run along the same general lines. We never observe the external world as such, instead, we observe certain incomplete aspects of it, and the nature of these aspects is determined by our mental equipment. We are able to grasp the space aspect and the time aspect of nature, and we have recently learned how to combine them into a more comprehensive aspect.

"This step was taken by Einstein and Minkowski,

but I do not think it goes far enough. Many physicists have been forced to use many dimensions, multiple causality, and multi-valued logic. This has resulted in a realization that physics deals entirely with *symbols* and can never reach the *substance* of the world. The only way we can describe the realities in the external world is by symbols which may be geometrical or mathematical. It is like the symbolic representation of a symphony by an arrangement of signs on a sheet of paper. A man born completely deaf could study the signs and the order in which they occur, but his organic defect would prevent his mind from grasping the essence of a musical symphony. If he were a mathematician, he might find interesting rules in the sequences, but with all his knowledge, he would be more ignorant about music than a small child with a sense of hearing.

"Coming back to the photons, I think it is highly significant that the light impulses from the different atoms in a source of light are not superimposed, for then we could not observe interference bands in fixed positions, like the ones we saw earlier in the evening. This lack of mutual interference was expressed in the statement by Nelson that a photon can only interfere with itself, a fact now generally accepted by physicists. Whatever it is that these wave systems represent in the external world, they appear to have a kind of individuality that overleaps time. It represents a case in which we can show, by physical methods, that something retains its integrity and individuality during motion, even should this motion be from a distant galaxy to an observer on the earth, and even if it should engulf a large portion of the universe. I have been told that the photons are a little frayed at the edges if they have traveled for many millions of years, and that is what we should expect."

"The last statement of yours must refer to the red-shift in the light from the extragalactic nebulae, and it may be all right," Nelson then remarked. "But for the rest I must say that if we follow the metaphysicians in their fanciful flight into unknown realms, we are soon lost in a fog of our own making. We know how light acts, and we can write down the rules for its activities, and these rules are sufficient for all practical purposes. It may be true that we never directly observe the external world in itself, but we can observe those of its activities which are of any importance to us, and these are the only things with which science is concerned. I have not the slightest interest in what a light beam is in itself, and I even doubt that such a question has any meaning. Right now I am interested in what a light beam does, and philosophers can talk until doomsday about what radiation is in itself without contributing anything to our knowlege about light. What we know about light we have learned from experimental physics and not from speculative philosophy. Perhaps a photon can jump from one place to another without moving along any definite path and be in many places at the same time, but I do not think Berman can do it. At any event, I certainly would like to see him try it."

Boris and Willard smiled broadly at this attack on speculative philosophy.

Berman, who was easily irritated, was delighted at the caustic remark. "I think if my friend Nelson would just put on a pair of scientific spectacles he would see me jump around and be in many places at the same time. Let me explain what I mean. In the first place, I claim that motion is a mental concept. In our mind we have a framework in space, by the aid of which we mentally locate our sense impressions in relation to one another. I do not see how anybody can know what location means in the external world, but we know well what it means within our consciousness and in our scientific models. If Nelson had eaten something today which did not agree with him, he might have seen me and the whole room move continuously to the right or to the left, or upwards or downwards, without getting anywhere, and he could have seen the same thing if he had taken or smoked certain drugs. We have all seen moving pictures in our dreams, which even if we had no other evidence would show that motion, *as we perceive it*, is a mental phenomenon.

"Our perception of motion is a combination of space and time elements, and in order to perceive a sequence in time with a difference between a forward and a backward direction we need a clock within our own consciousness. Expressed in physical terms, this clock can probably be pictured as an electromagnetic vibration with a nearly constant period, and we have reasons to believe that it is centered in the occipital part of the brain. This vibration, however, is itself perceived by our organ of space and time co-ordination and should therefore be regarded as a physiological manifestation of a more fundamental characteristic of our mind. Therefore, when Nelson speaks of my jumping from one place to another, he is talking about moving shadows in his own mind, and not about myself or my real activities.

"Turning now to the language of physics I want to call attention to the fact that if somebody would be able to see my body, it must be illuminated in some way or other, and the light must strike the observer's eyes and must be strong enough to stimulate the nerve cells in the retina of at least one of his eyes. Leaving aside for the present the difficult problem of how the light travels from me to his retina, we can all agree that light *acts* as exceedingly small particles, a fact well established by the photo-electric effect and by the Compton effect. Selig Hecht of Columbia University has recently shown that our eyes have been developed to such a high degree of sensitivity that a single photon can produce a perceptible sensation when it hits one of the rod-shaped nerve ends in the retina. Such faint stimulations often occur acci-

Expanding Waves and Small Particles

dentally, and we require the stimulation of several of these nerve cells to be convinced that the stimulation was actually produced by a light impulse.

"If our sense of vision were not influenced by accidental stimulation, and if it had a much greater resolving power in space as well as in time than it actually has, we would see a moving body as a group of scintillations similar to those we see in a spinthariscope or which anybody can see by looking with a magnifying glass on the self-luminous numerals of certain clocks. If Nelson's vision were perfect and not blurred, he would perceive me as a group of scintillations, which individually would come and go in an erratic way, each one appearing only for an instant. The group of scintillations may move, but he would never be able to determine with any accuracy where I was at any moment, since I would be scattered like a cloud of dust over a large area. When Nelson speaks about my motions, he means the motion of my body, and the only knowledge he has of my body has been acquired by the use of his sense organs, perhaps aided by scientific instruments. His refined observations would tell him that I am a cloud of luminous points that come and go. The points themselves do not move, but they jump from one place to another without traversing the intervening space, just like the moving pictures we see on a screen when the film is run very slowly. Now you can see what I meant when I said that if he put on his scientific spectacles he would really see me jump and be in many places at the same time."

"You may be right when you say that if I put on my scientific spectacles your body would appear to me as a group of erratic scintillations," Nelson replied. "But that would be my *perception* of your body. Your body, its cells, and its atoms do not come and go with the scintillations. I am sure you do not claim that if your body were in complete darkness, or if nobody were watching you, it would cease to exist. I therefore assert that the jerky motions you spoke about are the result of an illusion. I have often heard you say that the universe is in our mind, but you cannot convince me that, if all life in the universe were extinguished or if organic life never had been associated with a consciousness, the earth, the sun, the stars, and the atoms of which they are built would disappear. I think they would keep on doing exactly what they are doing now."

"I do not doubt they would keep on doing what they are doing now, but who can tell us what they are *really* doing?" Berman retorted. "When you speak about atoms you have in mind a complex of sensations and a model constructed from such sensations, aided by instruments, like microscopes, galvanometers, water drops in cloud chambers, etc. The model of atoms of year 1946 may differ greatly from that of year 2000, although I have no doubt it will be of the same general type, because the human way of thinking

Expanding Waves and Small Particles 61

does not change quickly in its fundamental aspects. But let us imagine a man on another planet who has inherited a quite different type of mentality. He may well picture each atom as having the same extension as the whole universe, since there is no limit to its gravitational field. He may not even think in terms of location, extension, separation, and duration, as we do, and if he and Nelson could exchange views about the properties, locations, dimensions, and motions of atoms, none of them would understand what the other was talking or gesticulating about.

"However, we can get around the limitations of our mind by describing the external world as a set of potentialities defining the place and the time where and when observable events of specified quality and intensity can be expected to occur. This is exactly what we do when we describe the formation of an interference pattern of light. Atomic models are very useful, but their main and perhaps their only purpose is to facilitate our predictions of observable events. With regard to the question of whether or not continuous motion takes place in the external world, I would say that all our measurements refer to discrete events separated by *finite* intervals in space as well as in time. Nobody has ever observed a particle moving in a continuous path, and I do not see what right we have to assume that in the external world there is anything of the sort. I think our idea of continuous motion is false, and that it has arisen because our sense organs are too crude to give us the correct idea of motion. With the introduction of highly sensitive scientific instruments we have learned about these imperfections, and I think the time has come to radically change our ideas about motion. It is good enough for animals, and it was good enough for our forefathers, but we have grown up and learned many new things, and we should adjust our imagery to correspond to our newly acquired knowledge."

Wilson, the philosopher, had been listening with the greatest interest and satisfaction to his friend's radical ideas about the external world and its inaccessibility to the human mind. He beamed with delight when he heard Berman's explanation of his idea about motion, and he realized immediately that it would be a great help in explaining the diffraction of electrons. But he was a man who liked to keep himself in the background. He thought Berman would be most happy if he found out for himself how important his remarks really were.

"I asked Willard to tell us tonight something about the diffraction of electron beams," Wilson said. "I think we are now ready to hear his account of a strange phenomenon which shows that electrons have wave properties in addition to their well known corpuscular properties. Mr. Willard!"

Willard was happy to make his report. "I became interested in the phenomena of electron diffraction for

Expanding Waves and Small Particles 63

a strange reason. This phenomenon appeared to me as a challenge to my common sense which has stood me in good stead in my activities as an engineer. If I am correctly informed there was an interesting dramatic touch to this discovery. Two research men of the Bell Telephone Company, Davisson and Germer, were studying the reflection of a beam of electrons by metals, and they used a polished piece of nickel as a reflecting surface. Nothing unexpected occurred, but something seemed to have happened to the nickel plate, which appeared to have lost some of its reflecting power as it was subject to the intensive bombardment by the electrons. The vacuum tube was opened, the nickel plate was removed, and then heated uniformly and slowly and again polished. When the experiment was repeated, it was found that not all of the electrons were reflected in their usual way, for some of them were apparently reflected in new directions, indicated by new intensity maxima in the photographic record.

"The investigators realized that the heating of the nickel plate had given it a crystallic structure. This induced them to replace the nickel plate by a single-crystal of nickel. Single-crystals of metals are made by melting a metal in an electric furnace and letting the solidification start at one point and spread from there, instead of letting the solidification begin at many points at the same time. When the single-crystal of nickel was used as a reflector for the electron beam, a regular reflection pattern was produced, and it was possible to measure with high accuracy the unexpected peculiarities in the reflections of the electrons by the crystal.

"At first no explanation for this strange phenomenon could be given. When the results were published, a German physicist called attention to the fact that a Frenchman, Prince Louis de Broglie, some years earlier by a combination of the quantum theory and the relativity theory had deduced that a moving electron should be associated with a wave system having a wave length equal to the quantum of action divided by the momentum of the electron. Very few scientists had taken de Broglie's suggestion very seriously. An analysis of the measurements by Davisson and Germer showed that they could be interpreted on the assumption that electrons had wave properties similar to those of light, and that the wave length was exactly as de Broglie had predicted. This was the beginning of the wave theory of electrons, a theory which later has been verified by other types of experiments.

"The discovery that electrons are propagated as waves of a certain wave length raises an interesting problem. Nobody questions the fact that electrons act as exceedingly small particles, but how can they be particles and waves at the same time or under different conditions? Evidently this problem is intimately connected with the similar problem concerning light, which as has been explained to us tonight can act as

Expanding Waves and Small Particles 65

waves and also as particles, now called photons. In order that you may understand the extraordinary difficulties in understanding this dual nature of electrons, let me describe a very simple case. We shall think of a beam of electrons passing through two narrow slits, side by side and very close together, an experiment very similar to that we performed with light at the beginning of this meeting. If we picture the electrons as very small particles, we must think of each of them as passing either through one slit or the other in order that it may reach the target. The interference of electrons tells us that each individual electron, in spite of its extreme smallness, does not go through one slit or the other, but it goes through both slits at the same time.

"If there were no interference between the two beams, each slit would produce its own image on the photographic plate, and although the images may well be superimposed to some extent, the effect would be quite different from that we actually observe which can be described as due to a superposition of waves and not of electrons. We can use the same language as Nelson did in the case of photons and say that an electron can only interfere with itself. We know that an electron cannot be divided, and we must therefore conclude that either the motion of an electron is just as much determined by the slit through which it does not pass as by the slit through which it actually passes, or else it does not *travel* at all in the form of a small particle although it *acts* as such. My common sense rebels against accepting either one of these alternatives. As I said awhile ago, this was the reason I became interested in this particular problem, which may have far-reaching consequences with regard to the nature of the external world."

"I have heard about the diffraction of electrons, but I have never been able quite to understand the nature of the evidence concerning their wave nature," Boris stated. "You just said that if an electron beam is reflected by a single-crystal of a metal, the electrons are reflected in several well defined directions. I suppose we can regard such a crystal as acting similarly to a system of exceedingly small mirrors or facets arranged in a definite pattern. One set of mirrors would then reflect a certain number of electrons in one direction, whereas another set of mirrors would reflect other electrons in a different direction, and so on. Can we not explain the way in which the electrons are reflected as the effect of a system of such elementary mirrors?"

"I think that this question must be answered in the negative," Willard replied. "In the first place, the directions in which the reflection occurs depend upon the speed of the electrons, which shows that the phenomenon cannot be regarded as an ordinary reflection of particles. This speed determines the wave length derived by de Broglie, and the reflections are defined by this wave length in the same way as light beams of

Expanding Waves and Small Particles

different colors are reflected by a diffraction grating. In the second place, when an electron beam traverses a very thin film of metal, we observe the same kind of ring system as is produced by light traversing a thin transparent plate, and the effective wave length is again that given by de Broglie's formula. I understand that there are many other reasons for assigning wave properties to electrons, but I am not competent to discuss them."

During Willard's explanation Berman became visibly agitated. As Nelson had expected, it had become clear to Berman that his idea of the nonexistence of continuous motion was in accordance with the interference phenomena in electron beams.

With a broad smile on his face, Berman said, "The diffraction of electrons seems to me to offer a verification of my contention that the science of physics is primarily concerned with a world of mental phenomena and does not describe the external world as such. When an electron does something, as when it causes the blackening of a grain in a photographic plate, our idea of it belongs to the world of our experience to a higher degree than does an electron which simply goes from one place to another without doing anything observable. Modern physics is trying to eliminate unobservable entities, and I think an electron in transit, as well as a photon in transit, belongs to this class. Ideas of unobservable entities are sometimes useful, even if everybody realizes that they are childish notions, but they should be dropped without regret if they lead to logical absurdities.

"Willard mentioned two alternative explanations, neither of which he was at all willing to accept. The first of these was that an electron moves like a particle through one of the slits, but that its subsequent motion is influenced by the presence of the adjacent slit. I suppose a defender of this hypothesis would claim that the electron is surrounded by an electric field, and that its field is divided between the two slits. Since an electron is known to be extremely small and cannot itself be divided, one would think that a larger part of the field would go through one slit than through the other, but in this case the effect would be blurred. The second alternative was that the electron *moves* like a wave system and not as a small particle, although it *acts* as a particle when it actually does something. The second alternative is more reasonable than the first, but I should like to express it in somewhat different terms. When we say that electrons travel like waves, we certainly do not mean that there are actual waves in an elastic medium, which travel from one place to another, like waves on a water surface. The waves are mathematical rather than physical, and they define where and when we can expect to observe an electron to become an observable entity. A wave is characterized by its shape, its length and its position, but its position is never exactly de-

Expanding Waves and Small Particles 69

fined at any one moment, and the peak of the wave defines the most probable position of the electron at any moment. The thing that travels can therefore be called a wave of knowledge concerning the momentary position of the electron.

"This knowledge is never exact, and the greater the wave length the less accurate is this knowledge. Since knowledge certainly is a mental thing, I am convinced that the propagation of electron waves is a construct of our own mind. I do not doubt that it has a counterpart in the external world, but I do not think our mind is able to grasp it. We describe this unknown element in the external world as motion, because our mind by its very nature projects our sensations on a frame work with space and time properties. I believe that space and time are themselves mental elements corresponding to some for us completely unknown qualities or aspects of the external world. Although they seem to separate events, it is easy to see that they also connect them. I even believe that my mind may well be able to communicate with other minds existing now, in the past, or perhaps even in the future, by means other than the electromagnetic distance effects characteristic for the science of physics. But I do not think we should discuss such questions now."

There were a few minutes of silence after Berman's speech. Everybody seemed to ponder the profound significance of the radical ideas expressed.

"I can agree with Berman that it is a kind of knowledge that is propagated in a beam of electrons or of light," Nelson said. "In fact, this is the opinion of many prominent scientists. Let me give a simple description of what is meant by such a propagation of knowledge. We shall imagine a ship moving towards a barrier in which there are two navigable channels, A and B. The pilot sees a channel and passes through it to the other side of the barrier, but he does not know whether it was channel A or B through which he passed. It is a dark night with overcast sky, and he can therefore not make any astronomical observations to determine his position. A storm is raging so that, although he knows the direction in which his ship is pointed, and its indicated speed, he cannot tell in which direction the ship is actually moving. The pilot asks the navigator to plot on the chart the ship's position and change in position from the available information. The navigator first assumes that the ship has passed through the channel A and draws circles on the map around this point on his chart, each of which represents a possible position of the ship at a given time. Then he does the same thing on the supposition that the ship has passed through the channel B.

"To simplify the procedure let us fix our attention to the circles which represent the ship's position at a particular moment after the passage. These circles, or rather limited arcs of them, represent equal probabilities that the ship is on some point on the circles at the moment considered. At one point the circles

Expanding Waves and Small Particles

cross, and this point represents a higher probability for the ship's true position than any other point on the chart. If there is an island near this point, the navigator knows that there is a relatively high probability of hitting the island, and he advises the pilot to change his course. As the night goes on, the uncertainty in the ship's position becomes greater and greater as indicated by the increasing length of the arcs. But then the sun rises, and through an opening in the clouds the navigator can determine the sun's altitude. This gives him a fix, and he draws a position line on the chart, and where this line cuts his circles corresponding to the time of observation, he regards as the correct position of the ship. If the line cuts the circle around A, but not that around B, he is sure that the ship actually passed through the channel A.

"In this example the ship represents a photon or an electron, and the two channels represent the two slits in a screen. The circles represent knowledge of position, and since this knowledge is not represented by a point but by a line, it is an imcomplete or partial knowledge. As time progresses the radii of the circles increase, and the circles expand at a rate corresponding to the speed of the ship. We may compare the expanding circles with two progressing circular waves, and where they intersect we have the well-known phenomenon of interference. The moving, combined wave system represents a progressing probability structure defining our knowledge, as well as the uncertainty in our knowledge, of the position of the particle at any particular moment. We can now replace the ship by bullets fired by a machine gun aimed at two slots in a wall, and some of the bullets go through the slots and in passing are deflected by unknown angles.

"This picture has often been used as an illustration of the propagation of a structure defining the chance that certain things shall happen at a fixed place in the future. We can then understand that, when the chance becomes a reality, the whole probability structure disappears instantaneously. This magical disappearance simply means that, as in a international lottery, the chance for everybody but the lucky winner disappears when the drawing has been made, and the disappearance is simultaneous for all the losers, even if they were scattered over the whole world. But beyond this the picture is an improper one. In the case of light, the effect of the two slits acting simultaneously is quite different from what it would be if the two slits acted independently of one another, as in the example given."

Wilson smiled a little when he said, "It is difficult for me to conceive of pure knowledge that goes up and down like a wave, and has a definite wave length, and can be polarized in different ways, as radiation is. If we use this picture we must regard radio waves as representing nothing but the chance of being able to listen to some radio program at a particular place and time. Although such an idea is logically unassailable, I doubt that many physicists would accept it. There is also another way of looking at these phenomena, which, I think, is more favored. According to this picture nature acts in definite ways, and particles actually move in continuous paths. In order to determine these paths observations are necessary, and the intrusion of an observer introduces an unavoidable uncertainty. An observer must use tools, and these tools are themselves made of particles, like electrons and photons, and no observation can be made without disturbing the system under observation.

"We naturally try to make this disturbance as small as possible, but there is a definite lower limit to the disturbance introduced. This limit is set by the quantum of action, since any interaction between two systems involves at least one whole quantum of action, and if there were no reaction we would obtain no knowledge. This leads to the so-called Principle of Uncertainty which works very well and never seems to fail. It seems to me, however, that this lower limit of interaction is applicable even if there were no observer at all, and we can hardly speak of knowledge without an observer. A photon that does nothing else than move from one place to another in our mental pictures and diagrams and does not interact with anything is a construct of our mind that cannot be verified by observation. It should be instantly dropped as pure fiction if it leads to logical contradictions, as it does in the present case."

Berman remarked, "An element of energy may disappear from an atom and later appear at another place with a retention of its characteristics, but in transit this energy is entirely in a potential form, a form that mathematically can be described as a field with certain structural properties. If we assume that there are moving particles guided by a field we must, as Dr. Wilson said, think of the energy as being partly in the form of a field and partly in another and more concentrated form. When the energy element actually does something, the effect is entirely in the concentrated form. Theoretical physicists object to a mixing of the two forms, and I therefore can see no reason why they should object to the assumption that an energy element in transit is *entirely* in the extended field form. It should be noted that the concentrated form can only exist for exceedingly short moments, represented by the time it takes a particle to act on our sense organs or instruments.

"I claim that both these forms of energy are constructs of our mind, and I admit that I do not know in the least how their counterparts in the external world can properly be described. I believe that it is precisely because motion is a construct of the human mind and describes a mental process, that this concept is not well fitted to describe what actually occurs in the external world. For why should all motions be associated with

Expanding Waves and Small Particles 75

waves of various length, and why should a mysterious constant which we call the quantum of action always be involved in our measurements?"

"I can agree with your ideas if applied to photons, but I cannot see how they can be applied to electrons," Nelson replied. "We have no reason to believe that radio waves carry with them any sort of photons, and since there seems to be no fundamental difference between electromagnetic waves of different wave lengths, I am quite willing to discard the idea of moving photons. But the case seems to be different in the case of moving electrons. Electrons act in two different ways. They can act by their extended electric fields, and they can act as small corpuscles, as when they hit the water drops in a cloud chamber. Further, the electrons have a mass that is not entirely due to their motion. Since an electric field is directly observable, I cannot understand how you can assert that an electron in transit is unobservable. It is probably true that if in our imaginary experiment with an electron beam passing through two slits we let the electrons do something when they are passing the slits, there can no longer by any interference of the two beams, but the electric fields in the beams are still produced by the moving electrons. I am unable to conceive of an electric field without the existence of any electrically charged particles."

Berman went on. "When we *see* that an electrically charged body is able to move another charged body in a certain way, we are not studying any external, moving bodies at all—we are studying certain moving pictures or shadows in our own mind. If we make our observations more refined and make accurate measurements with the aid of scales and clocks, we are, in addition, studying shadows of our instruments. The measured data have a physical significance with regard to the more exact behavior of a certain type of shadows in relation to one another, but the connection between this behavior and the processes in the external world are certainly indirect and incomplete. As I have said before, the pictures we actually see, with or without the applications of measuring instruments, consist of scintillations in our consciousness, each of which we can picture as being produced by a single photon stimulating a single nerve cell in the retina.

"The properties of electric fields are therefore derived from a study of a changing system of scintillations in our mind. We usually picture an electric field as being caused by electrically charged particles, but both the field and the particles are pragmatic ideas which may be useful, but must never be regarded as expressing any complete and true description of external events. We are therefore at liberty to modify our ideas, provided we do not introduce any conflict with the observed data within the frame work of the particular type of logic we have adopted. The classical picture of an electron surrounded by a field of

Expanding Waves and Small Particles 77

action, has been found to be inadequate for the description of interference phenomena, at least not without a very radical change in our ways of thinking. I prefer to think of an electron and its field as two different aspects of the same entity.

"The well-known physicist Sir James Jeans wrote in 1936 that 'we must move to some new plane of thought before we can realize that the particles and the waves are shadow pictures of one and the same universe.' The waves define a field, and this field represents a potentiality, and the electron is nature's own indicator of the existence and the properties of this potentiality. These two aspects never occur together, so that we can observe a field or its associated corpuscle, but never both at the same time. When the electron appears, its field of force disappears instantaneously, an idea in harmony with the instantaneous disappearance of a light impulse when a photon is absorbed.

"Conversely, instead of saying that an electron is emitted by an atom, we should say that a field of force or a wave system is travelling from one place to another, that is, travelling in our mental imagery and not in any external world, but there is no moving electron, since electrons and their fields of force, like photons and their wave systems, are mutually exclusive. An electron in transit should be pictured in our equations or diagrams as a field with space and time properties, whereas an electron in action should be pictured as a small corpuscle, a picture in accordance with our observations. Since from this point of view an electric field cannot be regarded as being caused by any particles, we must think of it as *autonomous*. It must have a cause, to be sure, but we should not regard the electron as this cause. It appears to me that the field defines in a statistical sense where and when we can expect an electron to appear, or rather the field is a construct of our mind created for the purpose of predicting the location and the time of an observable event."

"I cannot believe in fields that are not anchored in particles. Such fields are to me as incomprehensible as ghosts," Nelson said.

"They *are* ghosts in the same sense that radio waves are ghosts that have lost their association with matter." Berman replied. "The whole of nature is nothing but ghosts which act according to certain rules. The substance of the ghosts eludes our minds."

"Does it elude your brilliant mind too?" asked Nelson with a trace of sarcasm in his voice.

"It certainly does," said Berman. "But the realization of our ignorance is the beginning of a wider knowledge."

"I do not believe in anything supernatural," said Nelson.

"There is nothing supernatural about these ghosts," said Berman. "They belong to nature, and you can read about some of them in any text book in physics.

We notice the ghosts so often and are on such intimate terms with them, that we overlook the fact that we do not have the slightest knowledge of their intrinsic nature."

There was a short silence after this remark. The leader of the group thanked the members for their interesting remarks and declared the meeting closed.

CHAPTER 5

Vibrating Atoms and Exploding Bombs

Boris had heard from Berman that at the next meeting of "The Searchers" they were going to discuss the nature of atoms in general and atomic power in particular, and that a Dr. Charles Johnson, a research man who had participated in the development of the atomic bomb, would be present and would tell them something about nuclear physics. Just before the war in Europe started in 1939 Boris had heard rumors about the splitting of atoms, but then came a blackout of all information about nuclear physics. When the war with Germany started in 1941 he joined the Russian army as a fighting man, and he knew nothing about what was going on in the research institutes. He was startled when he heard about the atomic bomb dropped on Hiroshima in 1945, and he realized immediately that this was an event of the utmost importance which might well change the whole history of mankind.

After his telephone conversation with Berman and after his regular music lessons were finished for the day, Boris went to the Central Public Library to read up on the subject. He read some magazine articles and took home a copy of Smyth's report on "Atomic Energy." He read most of the book lying comfortably in bed. It was exciting reading, although part of it dealt with the technical difficulties encountered in the complex processes involved. From time to time the never-ceasing sounds of the activities in the great city reminded him that he was reading about a power that one day might stop all human activities in a small fraction of a second.

At the meeting Boris was introduced to Dr. Johnson, who was a man in his forties. Boris noticed that Johnson gave him a furtive glance when he heard the Russian name and learned that Boris had been in this country a short time only. Boris felt a little embarrassed, but he realized that in times of international tension, a scientist must be on his guard and suspicions are natural. With good grace he accepted his position in a situation for which he felt that he personally had no responsibility.

Wilson opened the meeting saying that they would discuss the properties of atoms and matter and the recent discoveries in the field of nuclear physics. He thanked Dr. Johnson for coming to the meeting and assured him that he was not expected to reveal anything that had not already been published in scientific journals and books or in reports from the government. "Before we go deep down into the hearts of the atoms," he said, "we must learn about their external parts, which have been the subject of investigation for many years. It was not so very many years ago since Rutherford found that an atom had a tiny nucleus that determined its properties. It was no wonder that it was hard to find the excessively small heart of the atom; it was like looking for a needle in a haystack. We need not go into the history of the ideas and of the discoveries of atomic properties, and we can immediately proceed with a description of the modern ideas of atomic structures. Our friend Nelson has promised to tell us something about these ideas."

Nelson looked around at the men sitting around the table smoking their cigars or their pipes, and began to talk as if he were at the desk in his classroom. "Our modern conception of an atom is based on the existence of small particles, which are the building blocks of atoms, just as the atoms are the building blocks of matter in general. The first discovered particle was the electron, which has a negative electric charge, always of the same amount, and an exceedingly small mass. The second kind of particle discovered was the alpha particle; they are emitted by radium and are identical with the nuclei of the atoms

Vibrating Atoms and Exploding Bombs 83

of helium. They have a positive electric charge exactly twice that of the negative charge of the electrons, and they have a mass nearly four times that of an atom of hydrogen. Hydrogen is the simplest form of atoms. It is built of an exceedingly small nucleus with a positive electric charge equal to that of the negatively charged electron. This nucleus is called a proton, and it has a mass about eighteen hundred and forty times that of the electron.

"Under ordinary conditions, hydrogen gas consists of molecules each of which is a combination of two hydrogen atoms, and its molecules are therefore built of two protons and two electrons. Under the influence of an electric discharge, some of the hydrogen molecules are split into atoms of hydrogen. The properties of the hydrogen atoms can be derived from spectroscopic studies of the light emitted, and in general most of our knowledge of atomic structures is derived from an analysis of the light emitted by the atoms under different conditions. Since there must be an electric attraction between the positively charged nucleus and the negatively charged electron, there must be forces which balance this attraction. In Bohr's model of the hydrogen atom the electrons are supposed to move in orbits around the nucleus, and the electric attraction is therefore balanced by a centrifugal force. This model reminds us much of the solar system, where the sun takes the place of the nucleus and the earth moves in its orbit under the influence of the gravitational attraction and the centrifugal force.

"The light emitted by an atom consists of pulses of electromagnetic radiation of definite frequencies, and the energy involved in any one of these pulses is equal to the frequency multiplied by a universal constant called the quantum of action. The energy lost by the atom in this process has always certain values, each one of which being represented by a particular spectral line. The same holds for atoms which absorb energy. The emission and absorption of light therefore involves definite changes in the energy content of an atom, and our pictures of atoms therefore consist of a system of levels of definite energy. We may compare our model of a hydrogen atom with a series of shelves of definite separation. When light is emitted and the atom loses a certain amount of energy, the electron falls down from a higher to a lower shelf; and when light is absorbed, the added energy lifts the electron from a lower to a higher shelf. When the absorbed energy reaches a certain amount, the electron is thereupon removed from the atom completely, which then is said to be ionized. It has then a positive electric charge, since the positive charge on the nucleus is no longer balanced by the negative charge of the electron.

"In the other chemical elements the nuclei are heavier, and their masses are approximately integral multiples of the mass of the proton. They have all positive electric charges which are exact multiples of the charge of the electron. When not subject to disturbing influences, the atomic nuclei are surrounded by a system of electrons of the same number as the number of unit charges on the nucleus, and the atom as a whole is then electrically neutral. The electrons seem to be arranged in layers around the nuclei, and the outermost electron or layer of electrons determines the chemical properties of the atoms. A description of the properties of the atoms would fill many volumes, but I hope this outline of our present ideas of atoms can serve as a starting point for our discussion."

Wilson, who well realized the difficulties of describing the complex structure of atoms in a few words, thanked Nelson for his presentation and invited discussion on the subject.

The critical Berman was immediately ready for his attack on the picture presented. In his somewhat aggressive manner he said, "Suppose a hydrogen atom is hit by another atom in such a way that the electron that moves around its nucleus is stopped in its motion. Would you not expect that the electron would fall down on the nucleus and form an electrically neutral body of very high stability? I have heard that such bodies are discovered and that they are called neutrons. Further, what prevents the system of electrons outside a heavier atomic nucleus from arranging themselves in other configurations than those you have mentioned? The electric forces alone cannot keep them in any unique, orderly arrangement, so far as I can see. And what is the cause of what we call electric forces?"

Nelson had often heard such questions raised by his students and he had always had difficulty in giving satisfactory answers. He said, "I can only state facts and do not attempt to explain why nature acts in this particular way. It is a fact that atoms emit and absorb light with definite frequencies, and that therefore their energy content changes abruptly and by definite amounts. I have not described the structure of atoms. I have been describing the structure of an atomic model, which can satisfactorily account for the observed behavior of atoms. Nobody knows the cause of electric or other forces in nature. As for the reason an electron does not combine with the oppositely charged nucleus, it might be that such combinations actually occur under exceptional conditions."

Johnson, the visiting physicist, remarked: "I do not think that neutrons can be an ordinary result of a combination of a proton and an electron. On the usual scale of measurements the mass of a proton is 1.0076, and that of a neutron is 1.0089. The mass of an electron on this scale is 0.0005. The combined mass of the proton-electron system is therefore less than that of a neutron. The mass of an atom or particle is a measure of its internal energy. If we stop the revolving electron, it loses energy, whereas the formation of a neutron would represent a gain in

Vibrating Atoms and Exploding Bombs 87

energy. In spite of the opposite charges of the proton and the electron, it requires energy to make them combine, as if there were repulsive forces at very small distances. In general, energy has a tendency to disperse, rather than to become more concentrated than it already is. The opposite transformation, namely a transformation of a neutron into a positively charged proton and a negatively charged electron, is associated with a release of energy and can therefore be expected to occur without external aid. Such transformations are assumed to be the cause of the emissions of electrons in spontaneous radioactive disintegrations. A proton can also be transformed into a neutron and a positive electron, but such transformation can only occur if a certain amount of energy is first absorbed."

Berman spoke again. "I do not think it is possible to explain the stable configuration of electrons in the atoms as an effect of attractive and repulsive forces, even if we assume a reversal of these forces at small distances. The system of energy level seems to me to be more fundamental than the electric charges. Do we really know with any certainty that the electrons actually move from one level to another?"

Nelson replied, "I agree with you that the system of energy levels is more fundamental than the positions and motions of the electrons, which, of course, are never directly observed. In fact, in the more advanced theories of atomic structures we no longer speak of moving electrons, which have been more or less dissolved into a 'cloud' of negative electricity inside each energy compartment. This method of representation has many advantages from a mathematical point of view, although it does not furnish us with a picture of the mechanism of the emission and absorption of light."

Boris had during the days preceding the meeting devoted much of his thinking to the structure and properties of the atoms. In his fertile mind an idea had begun to grow, an idea that at first startled him by its very simplicity. With keen interest he had listened to the opinions expressed, and he was particularly interested in the last statements by Berman and Nelson. He was also interested in the statement by Johnson that energy had a natural tendency to disperse, a fact he had learned in his study of thermodynamics, but never had he associated it with the transformations of atoms. He thought that he now had a good opportunity to find the reaction among the scientists present to his new ideas. He said: "Suppose that there are no electrons at all in the atoms, but only a complex field with a kind of cellular structure, and that therefore the structure of the field is entirely independent of the presence of any electrons."

Nelson showed his annoyance at this daring suggestion by the young Russian when he answered, "Without any electrons outside the nucleus there can be no negative electric charge to balance the positive charge on the nucleus. All electric fields are caused

Vibrating Atoms and Exploding Bombs 89

by electrically charged particles, often called corpuscles, with definite electric charge, positive or negative."

"If I understand you right in what you said a while ago," said Boris, "you described the cloud of negative electricity in a hydrogen atom as having a kind of cell structure, each cell having its own potential energy, and the electron as moving from one cell to another when the energy of the atom was changed. It seems to me that the only thing we really know about atoms are the values of its energy levels. I do not think we have any right to apply our ordinary ideas of matter to the electrons and other particles. Some people describe an electron as nothing but 'electricity', whatever that may be, or as a little piece of matter charged with electricity. It seems absurd to me that, if we claim that matter is always built of particles, particles can in their turn be built of matter."

Nelson was evidently irritated by the young man's arrogance, but he remained calm and said, "When we say that particles like electrons and atomic nuclei are material we simply mean that they have a mass and carry momentum, like matter in bulk. It has been suggested that the electrons themselves are built of some superfine substance, but nothing seems to be gained by making such an unverifiable hypothesis."

Wilson, the leader of the group, had been silent during this discussion. He was greatly interested in the problems raised, and in particular in the suggestion made by Boris. His philosophical mind pondered over the question whether we really had any right to speak about electrons existing in the atoms, that is, electrons as we know them by their effects on our instruments or on the water drops in cloud chambers. After all, what did we really know about electrons and other particles? Why did they sometimes act as particles and sometimes as waves? He realized that they were not prepared to discuss these problems, and he wanted to give their guest of the evening time to talk about nuclear physics.

He therefore stopped the discussion about the external properties of atoms by saying, "At our last meeting it was shown that electrons do not move from one place to another, and I suppose the same is true inside the atoms. But I do not think we can add anything to what was said then. I want now to ask our guest, Dr. Johnson, to tell us something about nuclear physics and about the recent development in this important branch of science. This development has led to the release of atomic power, a power which we, like Prometheus of the Greek mythology, in the most literal sense have taken down from heaven and have begun to use. Although it is sad to reflect that our first use of this power has been for destructive purposes, we can all hope that it will in the end be used entirely for the benefit of the whole human race. Some of us are not very familiar with modern physics and I hope therefore Dr. Johnson will explain the subject in as simple terms as possible."

Johnson responded at once. "Before the discovery of the neutrons in 1932 it was generally assumed that an atomic nucleus was built of protons and electrons, the former having a positive electric charge and the latter a negative charge of equal amount. Since the mass of an electron is very small, the number of protons determined the mass of the nucleus. This number, diminished by the number of electrons, gave the net positive charge on the nucleus. It is called the *atomic number* and is a characteristic for each chemical element. As Dr. Nelson has mentioned, the number of external electrons in an electrically neutral atom is equal to this atomic number. After the discovery of the neutron, a modified picture of atomic nuclei has come into use which has worked very well. In this model the nuclei are built of protons and neutrons. The number of protons defines directly the atomic number and determines the chemical and most physical properties of the element with which we are dealing. The sum of the number of protons and neutrons determines the mass of the nucleus and is called the *mass number*.

"For example, the nucleus of an ordinary iron atom consists of twenty-six protons and thirty neutrons, its mass number is therefore fifty-six, and the number twenty-six tells that it is iron. About ninety-two percent of all the iron in the earth's surface is of this type. About six percent of the iron atoms in iron ore have a mass number of fifty-four and contain only twenty-eight neutrons, and two percent have a mass number of fifty-seven and contain thirty-one neutrons. These are all stable elements, but there are other types of iron atoms which have smaller or greater mass numbers, and therefore contain a smaller or greater number of neutrons. These atoms are all unstable and last only from a few minutes to a month or two, but they can be observed when produced in a cyclotron or when iron has been bombarded by neutrons. As a general rule we can say that when an atom is abnormally light, that is, if the ratio of neutrons to protons is smaller than in the stable forms, it emits either a proton or an alpha particle, a process which increases this ratio, and the atom is changed to one of smaller atomic number.

"If an atom has too many neutrons for stability, it usually emits an electron, which results in a corresponding reduction in the ratio of neutrons to protons, but the mass of the nucleus is retained. We can picture this transformation as a production inside the nucleus of a pair of electrons, one of which has the usual negative charge and the other an equal positive charge. Such positive electrons, or positrons, have been observed in nature, but they exist in free form for only a very short time. It is therefore natural to assume that a positron inside an atomic nucleus im-

Vibrating Atoms and Exploding Bombs 93

mediately combines with a neutron and forms a proton, and the net result inside the nucleus is therefore a loss of a neutron and the gain of a proton. The negative electron escapes from the nucleus and can be directly observed. Spontaneous transformations are always associated with a loss in the mass of the nucleus corresponding to the energy of the ejected particles and the emitted radiation. Atomic energy is always dissipated, and in no case have we observed any spontaneous increase in the concentration of energy.

"Neutrons do not ordinarily exist in free form in nature, since they have a tendency to enter into combinations with all kinds of atomic nuclei. Neutrons are emitted by some of the lighter chemical elements when bombarded by alpha particles. The most common source of neutrons is a mixture of radium and beryllium, in which the alpha particles from the radium change beryllium atoms into ordinary carbon atoms, and high speed neutrons are emitted. By surrounding the mixture with a substance rich in hydrogen, the speed of the ejected neutrons can be reduced by collisions with the light atoms.

"A neutron has no electric charge, and it can therefore easily penetrate the cloud of electrons that surround the atomic nuclei in ordinary matter and effectively screen them from electrically charged particles of moderate speed. Neutrons moving in a material medium must therefore sooner or later hit an atomic nucleus. If they move very fast, they go clear through the nucleus, like a fast bullet goes through a window pane without shattering it. The wound in the nucleus, if I may call it so, is quickly healed, and no lasting effect is produced. If the speed of the neutron is reduced by collisions, it takes longer time for it to go through the nucleus, and its effects are then more profound. The neutron may stick to a nucleus, or it may cause the emission of particles of different types. Most important of all, it may split or shatter the nucleus, like a slow moving bullet may shatter a large window pane.

"In 1938 it was discovered that when uranium, which has the atomic number ninety-two, was bombarded by slow moving neutrons, the uranium nuclei were split into two parts of more or less equal mass with the emission of high speed neutrons and a large amount of radiation. This was an entirely new phenomenon and was called nuclear fission. It was later found that the fission did not occur in the ordinary uranium atoms, which have a mass number of 238, but in a particular type of uranium atoms having a mass of 235. This lighter type of uranium constitutes less than one percent of the more common type, and the proportion seems to be the same in all kinds of uranium ore. It was found that when uranium 238 is bombarded with slow speed neutrons, a new element of atomic number ninety-three and called neptunium was formed, and this element quickly changed into an element of atomic number ninety-four, now called plutonium. This element has properties very similar to those of uranium 235, but it has several advantages. First, it can be produced in greater quantity, since it is formed from the ordinary type of uranium. Secondly, since its chemical properties differ from those of uranium, it can be separated by ordinary chemical methods.

"In the fission of uranium 235 and of plutonium a few neutrons are released. If the speed of the neutrons is reduced, the released neutrons can themselves produce fission in new atomic nuclei, and the process then proceeds as in a chain reaction with explosive violence. The fragments of the fission, as well as the neutrons produced, are ejected at high speed. When the ejected particles collide with air molecules or with any kind of obstacles, they produce intense heat. This heat and the tremendous pressure waves in the air have an enormous destructive power which, as you well know, has been utilized in the atomic bomb. The high speed particles ejected also cause a temporary radioactivity in the area in which the bomb has struck, which has a lethal effect on all forms of life. Although so far we have only used atomic power for destructive purposes, there can be little doubt that in the future it can be used for the benefit of men. But it will take many years, I think, before we can reach this goal."

All had been listening carefully to what the visiting physicist had said. Although some of those present did not understand it all, they all realized the importance of the new discoveries.

After having thanked Dr. Johnson for his survey of nuclear physics, Wilson asked, "If uranium 235 is so easily split, I should think it would be unsafe to handle it or store it. Might it not explode spontaneously?"

"It can and does explode spontaneously," said Johnson. "Uranium is a radioactive chemical element, and in any mass of uranium some atomic disintegration always goes on, and a few neutrons are released spontaneously. If we have a relatively small amount of uranium 235 in one piece, only very few atoms will be split by the neutrons, since most of the neutrons will pass through the relatively very large interstices in the metal and escape at the surface. The number of effective neutrons would then be insufficient to sustain a chain reaction if it got started. But if we take a larger mass of uranium 235, how large I am not at liberty to say, a large portion of the neutrons released would be effective, the chain reaction would be started and sustained, and the whole mass would be blown to pieces. The methods used for setting off the atomic bomb is to bring together very quickly two pieces of uranium 235 in such a way that they form a unified mass. As soon as the pieces come together, the bomb explodes."

"I have seen the statement that a very high purity of uranium 235 is necessary, and that the purification

Vibrating Atoms and Exploding Bombs

offers great technical difficulties, since the mass of the effective uranium differs so little from the ordinary type," Nelson said. "Why is it necessary to have such a high degree of purity of the active substance?"

Johnson replied, "We are dealing with a very small margin of neutrons. Those neutrons which hit atoms of ordinary uranium would not produce fission, but would combine with the uranium atoms to produce neptunium and then plutonium. These neutrons would be useless so far as sustaining the chain reaction is concerned, and there would then not be enough neutrons to keep the reaction going. Further, many atomic nuclei have an affinity for slow neutrons, and even an extremely small amount of them would reduce the number of free neutrons below that needed to sustain the reaction."

Nelson continued, "Which is the more effective explosive, uranium 235 or plutonium? It has been stated that the bomb which exploded over Hiroshima was made of uranium 235, whereas the bomb used at Nagasaki was made of plutonium."

"I cannot say anything about their relative efficiency," Johnson explained. "Uranium 235 was produced first, but in the meantime we learned about the possibilities of plutonium. The latter can be produced in greater amounts from a given amount of uranium. The difficulties in producing plutonium are of a quite different type from those encountered in the production of uranium 235. In the making of plutonium they use big piles of pure graphite in which rods of metallic uranium are inserted. The graphite serves to slow down the neutrons, so that they can become effective. The reaction starts of itself, and the pile gets hot and must be cooled by enormous amounts of water running in pipes inside the pile.

"The whole thing is like a witch's kettle, or perhaps I should say the devil's cauldron. It requires careful control, and it is so potent that everything connected with its manipulation must be done by remote control. The pile emits neutrons, alpha particles, electrons, and gamma rays and exudes radioactive and therefore poisonous gases, and the operator must be protected by thick walls of cement. The action is regulated by moving rods of boron or cadmium in or out of the pile so that the number of released neutrons is just enough to sustain the reaction. A great variety of chemical elements are produced, some of them of very rare occurrence in the earth. The whole interior of the pile become radioactive, but in a week or so, the radioactivity dies down sufficiently, so that the stuff can be handled with relative safety, if proper precautions are used. The plutonium formed is recovered by chemical means and stored for later use. The stuff is radioactive and emits alpha particles, but it has a relatively long lifetime."

Everybody was impressed by the lurid description given by the scientist.

Vibrating Atoms and Exploding Bombs

After a while Boris asked, "Is there not a danger that the whole pile will explode like an atomic bomb?"

"I do not think that with proper precautions there is any danger," said Johnson. "But I do not advise anybody to play with it, and unauthorized experiments are prohibited by the government. The nature of the reaction in the pile is quite different from that in an atomic bomb. The reaction in the controlled pile is slow, whereas the reaction in the atomic bomb takes place in about a hundred thousandth part of a second."

"What would happen if the controls were completely removed?" asked Boris.

"If the controls were removed or if the cooling system did not work, the whole pile would melt, and when it came in contact with the air around the pile, the whole thing would burn up in a big bonfire. We can compare the pile with an old-fashioned charring stack, such as has long been used for making charcoal. These are controlled by regulating the inflow of air. If the air supply is insufficient, the stack goes out, and if too much air is allowed to enter, the whole stack burns up."

"I do not quite understand the necessity of bringing two pieces of plutonium together to start the chain reaction," said Boris, "Is it quite impossible to make a small atomic bomb?"

"I do not think it is possible to make a small atomic bomb," said Johnson. "We need a relatively large mass of plutonium to sustain the chain reaction. I can give an illustration from everyday life of the difference between the behavior of a small mass and a big mass of an active substance. Suppose we have a stack of hay which is not quite dry. Chemical action in the hay will set in and the hay will be hot. If it is a small stack, the heat will escape, and the temperature of the stack will reach a fixed value when the generated heat and the escaped heat are in balance. But if it is a very big stack, the generated heat cannot escape quickly enough, the temperature will rise, and the whole stack may burst into flame. In this case it is hot air that carries the heat from one place to another inside the stack, and this air travels very slowly. In an atomic bomb the energy is carried by neutrons from one atom to another, and this transmission is extremely fast. As only a big stack of hay can spontaneously catch fire, so only a big atomic bomb can explode, and its explosion is spontaneous. That is why we must bring two pieces of the active substance together to start the explosion. This must be done very quickly. In practice, a projectile of plutonium is shot against a target of the same substance. This takes place inside a heavy tube lined with graphite, and in the following explosion the whole tube evaporates in an instant."

Boris asked, "I have heard that the Germans were planning to use heavy water in their attempts to produce atomic bombs. What was the purpose of the heavy water?"

Johnson replied, "The heavy water was to be used for slowing down the neutrons and thereby make them effective in a chain reaction. A light atom is more effective than a heavy atom in slowing down the neutrons, just like a rubber ball rebounds from a yielding surface with a greater reduction in speed than from an unyielding surface. One would therefore expect that a substance rich in hydrogen would serve best as a moderator, that is as a material to slow down the neutrons. But ordinary hydrogen has a selective resonance absorption for neutrons of low speed, a property which the heavy hydrogen atoms also possess, but to a much smaller degree. The next atoms in the order of increasing mass are helium, lithium, beryllium, and boron, of which helium is the best, but it is a gas that does not enter in any chemical combinations and is therefore not suitable. Lithium and boron are useless, because these elements, particularly boron, absorb slow-moving neutrons. It is for this very reason that boron is used as a means of stopping and controlling the reaction in the piles. Beryllium is too scarce a metal to be taken into account. The next element is carbon, which although rather heavy has been found to act satisfactorily. It must be free from impurities, particularly boron, and graphite of high purity is therefore used.

"Heavy water would serve very well as a moderator, but a very large amount of pure heavy water is needed, and it takes a long time and great amounts of electric power to produce it. The Germans used the large hydro-electric plants in Norway, which had formerly been used for the fixation of nitrogen, for the production of heavy water. As soon as the British learned about this in 1942, they put these plants out of commission by heavy bombing. You can well imagine what would have happened to England and Russia, if Germany had been given an opportunity to develop an atomic bomb without interference.

"It may be of interest to you to learn that the first atomic chain reaction controlled by man was accomplished on the second of December, 1942. Before the reaction started, all but one of the safety plates of boron had to be removed, and when the last one was gradually pulled out in small steps at a time, the reaction slowly got under way. I do not have to tell you that the man in control, watching his instruments in a sheltered position, was relieved when he found that he could stop or diminish the reaction by pressing the button that by remote action pushed in the control plate. The first large pile went into operation in September, 1944, and in the summer of 1945 all chain reaction piles and other plants were performing satisfactorily. The first atomic bomb was exploded the 16th of July, 1945, in New Mexico."

Nelson said, "In the release of atomic energy a certain amount of mass must disappear, and the amount must be in accordance with Einstein's equation connecting mass and energy. Can a particle with a

Vibrating Atoms and Exploding Bombs

mass of a proton or a neutron be completely annihilated and its whole mass be directly converted into radiant energy?"

Johnson answered, "In atomic fission nobody has ever observed a release of energy of the intensity as large as that corresponding to the annihilation of a proton or a neutron. All the annihilated mass is in the form of what is called binding energy. The atomic particles are bound together with great forces of unknown origin, and the breaking up of those bonds accounts completely for the observed intensity of the released energy. Personally I doubt that any atomic particles, except electrons and positrons, can actually be annihilated."

Nelson went on. "I have heard it stated that in the hot interior of the sun atomic nuclei are actually annihilated, and that this is the origin of the heat radiated by the sun. What is the relationship between the heat generated in the sun and that generated in the atomic bomb?"

Johnson replied, "The theory of the annihilation of material particles in the interior of the sun has been found to be untenable. The accepted theory for the origin of the sun's heat is that suggested by Bethe and is based on well-established data. It states that carbon atoms combine with protons, and this starts a series of transformations which end in the formation of helium atoms, the carbon atoms being recovered in the process. The net result is a transformation of hydrogen into helium, and in this process a large amount of energy is released. This amount is considerably smaller than that produced by the complete annihilation of protons, however, and it is in fact less intense than that given out in the atomic bomb, although, of course, in the sun such transformations occur on a scale inconceivably much larger than that in an atomic bomb. Furthermore, in the sun the action goes on continuously, whereas in the bomb it is of extremely short duration. In other types of stars other processes must be assumed to account for the observed rate of heat radiation, but in no case have we any reason to believe that atomic nuclei are actually annihilated. It is fortunate, I think, that atoms are not annihilated, since otherwise an explosion like that of an atomic bomb might start to annihilate ordinary matter, and the whole earth might blow up in a blaze of glory in a fraction of a second."

Willard, the practical engineer, was particularly interested in the use of uranium as a new source of power. He said, "I understand that uranium is a fairly abundant chemical element. If this element can be used for the production of power, how would this new power supply compare with those we already have?"

Johnson explained. "Regarded as a general source of power the uranium in the earth's surface is *at present* less important than our coal and oil. The advantages of atomic power are that it can be extremely concentrated, can be shipped easily, and released quickly. It is therefore ideal for certain kinds of blasting, as when we want to dig a big canal, remove a mountain, or uncover mineral resources. The release of energy takes place in an inconceivably short time, and the resultant pressure and temperature are therefore enormous. But I think we could get the same amount of heat energy by burning some hundred tons of coal as from a pound of uranium, but the burning would take a long time and would be spread out over a considerable space. Our coal and oil may only last for about a thousand years, however. When this fuel is exhausted there is enough uranium and thorium to supply us with atomic power for perhaps a million years.

"The radioactive by-products are important in themselves since they furnish a cheap substitue for radium, in many respects superior to radium since the radioactivity is only temporary. It is obvious, however, that plutonium could be shipped to places where coal and oil are not available, and atomic power could then be made economical. As for the use of atomic power as a weapon, I am not competent to speak, but I feel that the existence of such weapons may act as a deterrent to any nation who wants to start a war. The sad part of it is, that a nation without a conscience would probably use it first, whereas a nation with regard for other peoples' rights would hesitate to use it, and would therefore be at a disadvantage."

Dr. Davis had been completely silent during the

technical discussion. He had thought much about the use of atomic bombs in future wars and of the dangers to civilization, if they were used by an unscrupulous power with little consideration for ethical values. He now asked:

"Do you think it was right of the United States Government to use atomic bombs on Hiroshima and Nagasaki in August, 1945? They were military targets, but a great number of people, who could not be regarded as personally responsible for the war, were burned to death or permanently injured."

"My personal opinion is," said Johnson, "that we should have first demonstrated the effect of the atomic bomb on a practically uninhabited place in the home islands of Japan. Later we could have announced our intention of bombing one or more places of military importance, stating the approximate time of the bombardment to give the population time to evacuate these places. It would not only have shown the Japanese our potential power, but it would at the same time have announced to the world that we do not intend to use the atomic bombs primarily for the destruction of human life. The objection raised to this course of action was that at the time we had only material for two bombs, and a 'dud' would have defeated the psychological effect on the Japanese government."

"I agree with you entirely," said Davis. "Love is the greatest power on earth, and without love mankind is doomed to utter destruction."

Boris listened with amazement to this statement by the old clergyman. It was obviously a very foolish opinion, or perhaps only a hypocritical statement, for he knew well that if you showed meekness towards anybody, he would lose his respect for you and take advantage of your apparent lack of strength or of desire to use it. He said, therefore, "I cannot see that you can get very far by love. It may be all right within your family or inside a small group, but if a whole nation showed love for its neighbors, it would soon be crushed by their more unscrupulous enemies and made to slave for them. Such things have happened many times in the history of the world, and human nature has not changed much. Love is personal, and it cannot be enforced by a police force."

Davis thought for a while and then said, "I would rather lose my life than my honor. An enemy can kill my body, but over my soul he has no power. It belongs to eternity. As for love being personal, I would say that love grows from understanding, and the governments can do much to promote understanding between nations."

Wilson, the leader of the group, realized that the discussion had taken a new turn, and he wanted to call attention to a subject of great importance to him. In a grave voice he said, "I am much worried about the serious consequences of an unrestricted use of atomic power, since it can so easily be diverted to atomic weapons. I approve of the American proposal for a world-wide compulsory inspection of all plants where materials for atomic power can possibly be produced. This condition is so vital that I understand many people in the United States would be willing to go to war and sacrifice millions of lives and spend many billions of dollars to secure it. We do not ask any privilege for ourselves which we do not grant to all other nations. I also think that the nations of the world should renounce the use of atomic power for a long time to come. Its use is of little advantage compared with the tremendous risk of its world-wide application. We can well wait until the nations of the world have learned to get along more peacefully, to understand one another better than they are doing now. The hourglass of the destiny of mankind is fast running out, and if we do not soon turn it around, it may be too late to save our civilization from disaster and perhaps total destruction.

"I am sure we are entering a new era in the history of the human race. I agree with Dr. Davis that in this new era mankind is doomed to destruction if we cannot raise the ethical level of all the peoples on the earth. It is a formidable and to some people an apparently hopeless task, but it is the most important one mankind has ever faced. Even our little group can exert its influence, not only in its fight against ignorance, but also in the struggle between good and evil. In my opinion a thinking man has greater potential powers than the greatest armies of the world. But his thinking and learning may debase him, if they are not coupled with love for his fellow men. If our actions are governed by selfish motives alone, the only laws of humanity will be those of the jungle, where you must kill or be killed. But I am sure that a higher power than that of man governs the world."

CHAPTER 6

Living Dust

AT THE next meeting of "The Searchers" they planned to discuss the problem of life. Berman had told Boris that Wilson was particularly interested in the origin of organization in animals, and that they could expect some animated discussion. Boris had studied some biology in school, but in college his time had been completely taken up with other studies. He was familiar with Darwin's theory of evolution, which he regarded as practically self-evident. He had admired Pavlov's investigations of the behavior of animals, and he had been told that a man's behavior was due to biochemical reactions. When animals reacted to a stimulus, it was nothing but a mechanical process, usually determined by some reflexes, which were themselves electrical or chemical phenomena. The complex structure of the animals was the result of a slow evolution from very simple organisms, and man himself was the product of this slow, evolutionary process.

Living Dust

Boris went to a public library and asked to borrow some books on biology. He was shown large shelves of books about plants and animals, and the magnitude of the subject at first overwhelmed him. There were so many strange words of Latin and Greek origin, languages he had never studied, and he realized that he would have a hard time learning their meaning. He took home some elementary books on biology and read them from cover to cover. He looked up the new words in his English-Russian dictionary, and the words he did not find there he could nearly always find in the big unabridged dictionary which he had bought in a secondhand book store and found extremely valuable. It did not take him long to become familiar with the new terminology.

He was an industrious reader, and he worked far into the nights to learn about the new science. It was not as difficult as many other subjects he had studied, although it required a good memory. His knowledge of physics and chemistry helped him greatly in understanding the books on physiology. He was particularly fascinated by the development of embryos, which stirred his imagination, and the thought of it kept him awake night after night. He slept a few hours in the mornings, but when he gave his music lessons he saw embryos developing before his eyes. In his dreams he heard a musical accompaniment to the development of an egg cell into an animal; it was a strange music with crescendos and diminuendos, beautiful accords and painful discords—and then the music stopped, and the animal was dead.

Before the meeting opened Dr. Wilson introduced a new member of "The Searchers." His name was Nils Anderson and he was an associate professor of biology in a college in the city. He was a big man with a ruddy, smiling face, a descendant of the Vikings. He had a hearty, thunderous laugh, and for him life seemingly was something to be enjoyed and never to be taken too seriously. He was a matter-of-fact man and a lover of outdoor life. His interest in biology had been aroused by his close attention to the animals and plants in the fields and forests he so deeply loved.

Dr. Wilson opened the meeting saying that the main subject of the discussion for the evening was the characteristic properties of life, and the origin and nature of these properties. "It is a big subject," he said, "and we can only discuss the most outstanding features of the phenomena of life. We are interested in its general aspects, and I feel that a knowledge of the many phenomena of life is necessary for an understanding of ourselves as well as of the universe around us. It is particularly the problem of organization which is of interest to philosophers. But we must first learn the facts, and Dr. Anderson has promised to tell us something about the progressive organization during embryonic development."

Living Dust

Anderson raised his bulky frame, for he liked to stand up when he spoke since he could then give more outlet for his nervous energy. Without any preliminaries he outlined the subject of embryology.

"When an egg cell is fertilized, it immediately forms two cells both of which have nuclei with chromosomes. The male germ cells, the sperms, and the female germ cells, the egg cells, have made equal contributions to the system of chromosomes in the fertilized egg cell. The chromosomes appear at a certain stage of cell division and look like threads or short bodies. They can then be made visible by staining the cell. They carry the hereditary qualities of the cell, although the fluid in the cell, the cytoplasm, also carries some hereditary characters. The chromosomes are built of proteins and contain an extremely large number of hereditary factors, called genes, arranged in a linear formation, like beads on a string. Some of these factors can be definitely localized in the chromosomes by studying the effect of bent or broken chromosomes.

"The egg cell divides a great number of times until a little ball of cells is formed. This later becomes hollow and is now called a blastula. In animals the blastula caves in at a certain point, and then forms a cup which is called a gastrula. Its opening is sometimes called the primitive mouth, but most biologists call it the blastopore, which means the opening to the germ. The general organization of the animal seems to be due to something at the edge of the blastopore. In the formation of the gastrula this organizing substance is transferred to the inner, dorsal wall of the gastrula. In vertebrates the spreading influence can be observed as a formation of a string with adjacent structures, although this string does not become visible until a somewhat later stage. This string is called the notochord, and it induces the formation of nerve tissue in the rapidly developing embryo. This is nerve tissue which later forms the brain, the spinal cord and the nervous system, and it seems to be responsible for the general organization in vertebrate animals. The hereditary elements in the chromosomes, the genes, determine structural *details* in the animals, whereas the *general* organization seems to be determined by something else, which in potential form seems to reside in the dorsal lip of the blastopore."

Everybody in the group showed great interest in the biologist's short description of the embryonic development of an animal. Boris' eyes shone with a strange light, which astonished his friend Berman.

Dr. Wilson thanked Dr. Anderson for his brief summary of the development of an egg cell, and invited discussion.

Willard, the engineer, was the first to make inquiries. "What is it that makes the hollow blastula cave in and change into the cup you called a gastrula? I understand that this process takes place in nearly all animals, and there must be a very definite reason for this phenomenon. And how can you speak about a dorsal side in an embryo which has no front or back?"

"I shall answer the second question first," Anderson said. "When we speak of the dorsal and ventral side of an embryo, we are simply referring to those parts which as we know from experience later become the dorsal and the ventral side of the animal. The first question is difficult to answer. We may compare the motions in a gastrula with the motions in an amoeba, which changes its shape in order to propel itself. It is a concerted activity, proceeding according to a certain plan. It has a definite goal, which seems to be to place the organizing substance in a definite position relative to the cell material, which will later develop into the brain and the nervous system. It is interesting to note that when a piece of the gastrula is transplanted into a different region, for instance into the central cavity of the embryo, it keeps on for a while changing its shape, in the same way as it would if it were in its original position. I do not think anybody knows what causes the motions. A physicist is satisfied when he knows how an electric field acts, and he does not pretend to know why it acts in this particular way. When an animal moves its legs, we do not usually look for an ultimate cause, but are satisfied when we can understand the mechanism involved."

Everybody understood that the explanation was far

from satisfactory, but it was not so easy to see why the motions in a gastrula were more mysterious than those of animals in general.

Berman realized one important aspect of the phenomenon. He said, "The contraction of the muscles of my arms and legs is associated with nervous impulses, in some way caused by an action of my will. I have never heard that anybody has observed any nerves in an amoeba or in a gastrula, and it is hard to imagine a gastrula with a conscious will. The difference between the motions in an amoeba and in a gastrula seems to be that the motions in the latter always occur only once, and then they follow a definite predetermined pattern common for all animals. Perhaps we may compare the concerted motions in a gastrula with those occurring in a heart, although in the latter case the motion is periodic. The pulsation in a heart muscle is also common for a large class of animals, and some sort of circulatory system may be essential for all types of life. The beating of the heart is regulated by nerves, however."

"The regulation by the nerves of the heart muscle has been extensively studied," said Anderson. "Certain nerves make it beat faster and other nerves make it beat slower. It is interesting to note that if we place a piece of the heart muscle in a tissue culture and keep it alive, the cells have a tendency to pulsate. The function of the nerves, therefore, seems to be to co-ordinate and regulate the inherent tendency to pulsation in such a way that the whole heart acts as a unit. In the gastrula we have an example of co-ordinated motions without any nerve system; at least, there are no visible connections which can take the place of a nerve system."

"This is extremely interesting," said Berman. "In the gastrula we have evidently a striking example of co-ordinated motions, always executed along the same general plan, and without the aid of any visible, co-ordinating agency. If we encountered such phenomena in the inorganic world, we would say that they were due to a field of force, a field in which the lines of force followed a certain fixed pattern."

At the mention of a field of force Dr. Anderson showed signs of uneasiness. He was a mechanist in his conception of biology, and a field of force regulating special vital processes smacked too much of vitalism, which was anathema among well-informed biologists. But the idea could not be brushed aside as the fantastic speculations of an amateur, for even professional biologists of the highest standing had had the same idea. So he decided to retreat and take up a well-fortified position.

"The notion of an organizing field of force was introduced some years ago by Hans Spemann," he said. "It seems to be a good picture for describing the cause of concerted motions, but a field which does not have its origin in atoms is unthinkable. Field and matter are intimately associated, and a field which is not determined by matter has no rational basis for its existence. It would be as unreasonable to think of a field without material support as to invoke a genie from nowhere, compelling the particles of matter to move along certain paths. If we admitted the existence of such spirits, biology would become an irrational science, and no scientific program would be possible."

Berman and Nelson exchanged a glance full of meaning. They both remembered the verbal duel they fought at the last meeting, and they were eager to renew the fighting. Nelson was sure that he could obtain valuable aid from the biologist, and Berman was eager to show that his idea of the autonomy of force fields could be substantiated by biological phenomena, even if Anderson, the representative of biological science, was hostile to his ideas. For Berman the organisms described in biology were moving shadows in the human consciousness; they were symbolic of something far transcending the atoms and the molecules of the science of physics.

"Do you claim," Berman said with some heat, "that the motions in the embryo during the formation of a gastrula are wholly due to the molecular properties of the cell substance, and that all living organisms owe their structure and structural changes to electrical fields produced by the configuration and motions of the electric elements in the molecules, in accordance with our usual physical theories? How have the molecules then acquired this convenient arrangement?

Our brain, our nervous system, our skull, and our whole body, do they owe their structure to the molecules of which they are built, and ultimately to the molecular structure of the human germ plasm? Does the structure of the chemical substances in our body and in our germ plasm satisfactorily explain the functions of our organs and our ability to see and feel and, above all, to think?"

Anderson was not prepared for questions of this profound character. He had heard them before, but seldom in scientific gatherings, and never had he heard them expressed with such zeal. With a wry smile he answered the doctor. "Those are far-reaching question which are easy to raise, but difficult to answer. Biologists know well that their science is still largely descriptive and not explanatory. Certain phenomena can be explained in the same way as a physicist and a chemist explain phenomena in their respective sciences. The application of physical laws is of a tremendous help in physiology and medicine, and we intend to use mechanistic conceptions to the very limit of their applicability, and not introduce extraneous ideas until every other method has definitely failed. As long as we use established physical laws, we know that we are on safe ground, and I hope we shall never have to introduce mysticism into the science of biology. All of the arguments against a mechanistic concept of life have been shown to be invalid."

"I definitely challenge this last statement," Berman said. "The most fundamental objection against mechanistic biology is that it gives no explanation of organization, of structure, of functions, or of consciousness itself. Can you honestly say that you believe that the structure and function of your brain are entirely determined by its atoms and molecules?"

"I admit that I do not believe it," said Anderson. "But the only thing I can do about it is to study how the brain works and to wait till we get more facts. If we speculate without enough facts, we are following preconceived notions, and there is then little chance of finding the truth."

Dr. Wilson had followed the discussion with great attention. He did not have the aggressive enthusiasm of Berman, but his clear, logical mind made him see things in a detached, impersonal way. He knew well the weak points in modern science and wanted to bring them out clearly.

"There are certain fields in science," he said, "where it is not so much increased knowledge of facts that is needed, but rather an unbiased and courageous thinking. The structure and the functions of our brain and nervous system, for instance, can not in my opinion be a direct result of the molecular structure and composition of the matter involved. This structure is inherited, and Dr. Anderson has just told us how it emerges from a certain region in the embryo and gradually develops into our nervous system. The potentiality of this system must exist in some form in the embryo, and the question before us is how we can picture this form and its subsequent development. Some hundred years ago there were biologists who believed that in the sperm cells there were extremely small replicas of the complete animal, called animalcules, but we know now that this is not the case.

"The only way I can picture this potentiality is in non-physical terms, that is, as a source which itself has no structure, but is capable of producing a guiding field which can arrange the atoms and molecules into the pattern we see with our eyes. This idea was developed by the great biologist Hans Driesch, but his ideas were rather vague and were not received with favor by his colleagues. Spemann's idea of a guiding field appeals to me. This field must have an origin with a definite location in the embryo and must possess potential properties. This idea is not so fantastic as it looks at first sight, because all the fields of force of which we have any knowledge have well-localized sources. In an electric field we have positive and negative elements of extremely small size, and the electric fields are usually supposed to be anchored in such points. Electrons have very small inherent mass, and I can very well imagine a field in which the source have no rest-mass at all, that is, they are immaterial."

Nelson, the physicist, had been silent till now, but when the subject of the discussion turned to a field familiar to him, he joined in the discussion. "An immaterial source of a field of force is not a concept which physicists can accept without strong evidence. The field of which Wilson speaks must grow in size and have a certain energy content which changes with its size. Further, a mass-less source has no energy and is therefore unobservable, and we have had enough of unobservable elements in physics."

"I know that physicists do not like unobservable elements, but I know also that many of the elements of which they speak are themselves unobservable," Wilson replied. "Nobody has ever seen an electron; what we observe are certain effects registered by an instrument or by our sense organs. Electrons are constructs of the human mind, very convenient, to be sure, but they are nevertheless invented by us. Are we not permitted to invent other elements to explain another class of phenomena? After all, we are always talking in terms of allegories adapted to minds similar to our own. We say that nature works as *if* there were electrons, particles and atoms, but we are all the time talking about ideas, conforming to the particular type of mind we possess.

"With regard to mass-less particles, may I remind my learned friend that physicists speak of radiation as a stream of photons, the mass of which is entirely due to their motions. According to accepted theories of the increase of mass with velocity, they have no mass of their own, and if we could think of a photon at rest, it should have no mass at all. As to the energy needed for the field to expand and grow, it seems to me that this can come from material substances."

Berman was now greatly excited. He understood immediately the far-reaching consequences of Wilson's suggestion, and with his knowledge of physiology he saw also where the energy would come from. He jumped to his feet. "This is a very interesting idea," he said. "It may not be new, but I see it can explain many things, which cannot be explained in any other way. We have all heard of the hormones which stimulate the growth in plants, and which can for instance, make roots grow from any part of a plant. Other hormones are acting during the development of embryos, and some hormones are secreted by the endocrine glands and stimulate the activities of our organs. I know that some biologists speak about morphogenetic hormones which are supposed to be chemical substances that determine the embryonic development. How can a chemical substance determine the structure of my skull and my brain? I would rather think that these hormones carry energy of a highly specialized form and actuate inherent, form-producing potentialities."

"I do not think that a chemical hormone can by itself determine the structure of the human skull and brain," said Anderson. "But it seems to be well established that there is, for instance, a head-producing hormone which appears at a certain time and place in the development of an embryo. There are also hormones of a more general type which can start the development of any part of an animal. These so-called organizers are probably relatively simple chemical substances, and I can see no objection to regarding them as carriers of energy. The ultimate cause of the organization in animals is unknown, as I have said before, but I believe that it is entirely mechanical."

"The word mechanical may mean many things," said Berman. "When I move my arm it is a mechanical process in the sense that there is a change in the shape of certain muscles, and the law of conservation of energy as well as other physical laws apparently hold. But other factors are also involved. For instance, we know that, at least in our own bodies, there is often an action of the will, which we certainly cannot regard as a physical process. But coming back to the specific hormones, I have an idea which may be of value. If there are living fields determining the structure and function of our developing organs, any part of such an organ contains a part of the field. This field is stabilized by the incorporated molecules and can therefore be transferred from one embryo to another. The field represents a frequency pattern, and the molecules have formed a structure in which their vibrations conform to the inherent vibrations in the living field. I can well imagine that if we cut out a piece of that part of an embryo which is developing into a head, and transfer this piece to another embryo, it can, simply because of its inherent pattern of frequencies, induce the formation of a head in another embryo, provided, of course, that the head-producing potentiality is already present in the second embryo at the place where the transplantation occurs. This would explain many of the transplantation experiments by Spemann and his associates."

Anderson said nothing about the strange idea of Berman. But Boris, who knew so little about biology, suddenly came to life. He had been in a state of concentrated thinking; he had heard what was said, but his mind was turned inward, listening to the same music he had previously perceived in his dreams and which accompanied the development of an embryo. Hesitatingly he started to tell about his visionary thoughts, but soon his confidence asserted itself, and looking out into empty space he described his strange ideas. "The frequency pattern of which Dr. Berman speaks reminds me of a melody. It is the 'symphony of life.' When the atoms dance to certain tunes we say that they form a living system. Physicists call such phenomena resonance, and by this they mean that matter can be set in vibration by energy of certain frequencies. The melody of life is not a pattern in time, like those we hear with our organs of hearing. It is a symphony in space as well as in time. The symphony has its crescendos and diminuendos, its repetitions and variations, both in space and in time, and we observe it with our eyes as changing structures where certain standard patterns are repeated.

"Behind the symphony of life there is a universe in action, a universe not built of atoms and molecules. We can perceive it with our senses other than vision, for it gives us the life we feel in our bodies. It gives the purposeful organization we see in animals and plants, it is the ultimate source of our feelings, our will and our thoughts. We are only conscious of certain accords in this symphony, and it has a deep meaning of which we only know a small part. I do not know where the melody comes from, but there is beauty in it, and there is an intelligence far surpassing our understanding. When I see a flower I see an accord spread out before my eyes, and when my mind feels the symphony behind it, I perceive the essence of life."

Boris suddenly stopped his eloquent speech. Never before had he expressed such sentiments. He had always spoken the language of a matter-of-fact man. He was a poet and a visionary at heart, but he had never realized it before. He knew well that music gave him a feeling of being detached from the ordinary world, but he had never before realized that there was a music in the world of his everyday experience.

Nobody said anything for a while. Some of those present felt as if a fresh wind from another world had swept away a fog and cleared their vision and revealed a vibrating life, hidden behind the dust on which their eyes had been focused. Others felt, however, that this was no way for a scientifically educated man to speak. Only starry-eyed mystics or ignorant fanatics could be expected to express such ideas. But they all admired the courage Boris had shown.

Anderson, who knew nothing of Boris' character and ability, was the first to express an opinion. "It seems to me," he said, "that Mr. Charkoff's theory of life could best be used as a basis for a fine poem or symphony, but as a scientific explanation it is of little value. Life is not a symphony, it is a play of forces, probably the same as we meet in all kinds of matter. Mr. Charkoff's ideas have been expressed before. Calling life a symphony does not help us to understand the physiological processes, it does not help us to produce greater or better crops, and it does not help us to cure diseases and to improve our health. On the contrary, it scientists were satisfied with such ideas, there would be no incentive for serious research, because they would have to give up all hope of understanding the origin, development, and nature of life. The only good such theories could do would be to give visionaries a sense of pleasure, and preachers some new themes for their sermons."

Dr. Davis had been quietly listening to the discussion. He was highly surprised and pleased with Boris' idealistic conception of life. When he heard the biologist's denunciation, and the allusion to visionaries and preachers, he felt it his duty to defend the position of the idealists. "I know that there are scientists," he said, "who think that their researches have no other value than their utility for the material development of mankind. This is a natural point of view among primitive people struggling for food, shelter, comfort, and health, and sometimes for conquest and domination. But research should also be a quest for truth for its own sake. We have all seen the immediate value of scientific discoveries, but I believe that the greatest value of these discoveries is not of a material nature. When science has determined the structure of an atom, of a vitamin, or of a living cell, the discovery is of practical use for all mankind, but as it says in the Bible, 'man does not live by bread alone.'

"There are spiritual values of far greater importance than food and comfort, important as these are for our daily life. The facts science discovers are symbolic of eternal verities. They are like the shadows we see on the screen in a motion picture theater, their value is not in the arrangement of the dark and bright patches, but in the ideas they evoke and the feelings they stir up in our own minds. The shadow-plays in our minds, to which Berman has called our attention, and which we call the physical world and which the scientists study in great detail, are symbols of beauty and harmony, of meaning and intelligence. Therefore I think Mr. Charkoff's description of life as a symphony shows a greater insight into the mystery of life than biologists can ever attain by their study of the shadows of life. Personally I regard the symphony of life as emanating from God, the ultimate origin of all things."

Berman was impatient in his desire to defend his friend Boris, and he could hardly wait for the clergyman to end his talk, interesting though it was from many points of view. Looking at Anderson, he said, "Suppose I told you that in a desert I saw a whirling cloud of dust, which gradually took the form of a man. It walked on two legs, it had two arms and a head with eyes staring at me. It shook hands with me and talked intelligently like an ordinary human being. I photographed its body with an x-ray camera. All the bones were in their proper places, the organs were functioning properly, and the blood circulated in its usual way. Then the cloud disintegrated, and there was nothing left but a heap of dust. If I told such a story you would certainly think that I was crazy or had had a bad dream. But this is a true story, and you yourself have seen something very similar happen.

"The transformation of dust into a man does not occur in the air, but in water, and the dust particles are taken in as food containing certain chemical compounds. In a general way, however, the picture I have given represents the formation of a man. It is therefore perfectly legitimate to say that the organization in animals does not originate in its atoms and molecules, but must come from other sources. Mr. Charkoff is a musician, and he naturally compares an arrangement ordered in space and time with a symphony. I may even agree with Dr. Davis that such an idea goes deeper into the foundation of life than any theory advanced in biological textbooks.

"In support of the idea of the existence of a 'Symphony of Life' may I call attention to the recent discovery made by investigators in the Section of Neuro-Anatomy of the Yale Medical School of complex, electrical fields within and around all living organisms. These fields are specific for the species and are particularly active during embryonic development, when they extend beyond the boundary of the embryo and determine its future development. At death the fields disappear. Dr. Burr, the leader of the group who is making these investigations, states that it is hard to avoid the conclusion that the electrical pattern is primary and to some extent at least determines the morphological pattern. In other words, the observed field is apparently not produced by the atoms and molecules in the organisms; instead it determines by its own innate properties the structure and the future development of the organism through its action on the proper kind of building material.

"It can therefore well be described as a living, autonomous, and organizing field of force. There can be little doubt that such fields are dynamic rather than static, and that fundamentally they are built of vibratory elements somewhat similar to those we assume to exist in atoms. If we could convert the electric vibrations into audible sound waves, as we do in our

Living Dust

radio receivers, we could directly listen to some of the accords in this symphony of life. The essential thing is that these organizing fields are well-ordered and fine-grained and have such a marvelous internal structure that they can transform 'a heap of dust' into a living man. I am convinced that those living fields which are responsible for the structure of our brains are intimately connected with our own consciousness."

Anderson was somewhat surprised at the poignant speech of his opponent. He knew well that he had a difficult position to defend, but all his training had been based on the immutable laws of physics and chemistry and their application to biological phenomena. Considerations of electrical fields acting independently of atoms were abhorrent to him. Expressions like 'the symphony of life' reminded him too much of the flowery speeches and the soporific sermons he had heard from the pulpit, when as a boy he was forced to go to church with his parents.

"The thing that causes the organization in an animal," he said, "is something in the fertilized egg cell, but what it is and how it acts is hard to say. But we have organization even in inorganic matter. A crystal consists of a great number of atoms, arranged in a definite pattern. A crystal is formed from moving atoms and molecules and can be formed from matter in solution, or in a molten or gaseous state. We may well regard a crystal as a form of organized dust, as you call it. The organization is much simpler than in living substances, but if matter can organize itself in simple forms, there should be no great difficulty in regarding the organization in living matter as of the same type as that in inorganic matter. Some viruses actually seem to be living crystals."

Berman's answer to the biologist's contention came immediately. "The molecular arrangement in the crystal is not an organization of the same kind as that in the living world. It is rather a repetition of a pattern inherent in the molecules themselves, and a crystal is really a large molecule. The structure is determined by the electrical fields in the atoms, and in crystals there certainly are no organs performing the different functions necessary for the continued existence of the structure. If we regard life as a symphony, atoms and crystals are individual tones. A symphony consists of individual tones, and organisms of atoms and molecules, but a symphony is more than a mixture of tones, and an organization is more than an aggregate of molecules.

"Further, in all living organisms there occur chemical changes necessary for the various processes of life. These processes are manifested in the digestion and the assimilation of matter for the maintenance and growth of the organism and are followed by elimination of waste products. This metabolism in all living matter may be temporarily suspended, but as soon as the conditions become right, and provided the organism can survive the suspension of its metabolism, the normal processes of life begin anew. We are all familiar with this in the development of seeds. Life can therefore exist in latent form as a system with well coordinated functions and structures in a potential form. Here lies, I think, the fundamental difference between living and non-living structures. The viruses Dr. Anderson mentions may chemically be protein crystals, but this does not prevent them from having a structure that is not entirely dependent upon the field of the molecules involved. There are dead proteins as well as living proteins."

Wilson, who had first suggested the existence of living guiding fields emerging from vital sources in living organisms, was now ready with a further elaboration of his idea. "From Berman's last statement it occurs to me that the guiding fields which determine the structure and functions of living matter have definite developmental pattern, but the scale of these patterns can vary both in space and in time. The field or pattern can therefore have a location but a vanishingly small size, or perhaps no size at all, in the egg cell, and a relatively large size in a fully developed animal. Its rate of development or expansion can actually be zero, as in a seed in the absence of moisture or of oxygen, and it can be very large, as in the growth of a mushroom. The pattern has a time structure as well as a space structure, and the scale of both these structures is different under different conditions. The direction of the development may even be reversed, at least the space scale can diminish as well as increase. This, I think, is what happens at death, when the space scale of the living guiding field diminishes and shrinks to a point. This gives the ordinary physical forces of the molecules a free play, and the result is a quick disintegration of all fluid structures.

"Boris' idea that life can be compared with a symphony with a space structure in addition to its time structure is of great interest to philosophers. Life, as we see it with our eyes, is nothing but a shadow picture in our mind. The shadows have certain standard patterns, like those in the organs, the cells, and the chromosomes. We say that the life we observe in this way belongs to the physical world, because its structure in space can be observed by many people, and therefore differs from a structure we see in dreams and hallucinations. A symphony has also a definite structure that can be perceived by many people at the same time, and it can be preserved on a phonographic record, just as a space structure can be recorded by photography. A symphony heard with our ears and an animal seen with our eyes are both structures in our mind, and they are both symbolic of something external to ourselves. But a record of the symphony is not the symphony itself, and the photograph of an animal is not a living animal.

"The symphony I hear is more fundamental than the symphony recorded on a plate or the symphony represented by the vibration in the musical instrument and in the air. Behind the symphony that a musician hears, there is beauty and there is meaning. If we apply this idea to the shadow pictures of animals and plants we perceive in our consciousness by the aid of our organ of vision, we can well understand the fundamental truth of Boris' idea. When biologists study life, they are so engrossed in the study of structural properties, which include all physical and chemical properties, that they forget to listen to the symphony of life. This is the real essence of life, and the structural properties are symbolic shadows of this essence. It requires a special gift, akin to that of a poet or an artist, to hear this cosmic music of life and to realize its significance."

Anderson did not respond to the last part of Wilson's speech. But he felt that he should object to the idea of expanding and contracting living fields. "If these living fields can expand and contract," he said, "and can have location without size, I would like to know where they are before the egg cells were formed, and where they are after death. The field in an egg cell before its formation presumably would be somewhere in the ovary, and before it was in the ovary it was in the egg cell from which the individual was originally formed. Its origin is pushed farther and farther back. Where did it come from when it first made its appearance on the earth? And at death, the field which according to your theory seems to have an autonomous existence, where does it go to? Or does it vanish like a symphony when the music stops?"

Wilson thought a little and said: "These are problems of great importance and I do not think we are prepared to discuss them tonight. They are intimately connected with the development and origin of life and of mind. Without any definite ideas about the origin and nature of our own mind it is impossible to analyze our knowledge of life and its origin. I therefore suggest that at our next meeting we discuss the nature of the human mind and its relationship to our bodies. I hope nobody will feel offended if unorthodox ideas are expressed. After all, it is only by studying all possible theories that we can arrive at the truth."

Boris walked home with Dr. Berman. He was in deep thought and Berman did not like to interrupt his friend's reflective mood.

After a while Boris said, "I wonder what came over me tonight. Never before have I talked in this way, and I felt as if somebody else had spoken through me. I am sure my friends in Russia would entirely disagree with the unscientific opinions I expressed. You are a psychologist and perhaps you can explain my actions."

"There are many things we cannot explain," said Berman. "Personally I think you were inspired by a new idea which appealed to your subconscious thinking. You certainly gave them something to think about. You were grand."

Boris thought a little and said, "It may be all right

to compare life with a symphony, but what good does it do us? I think Anderson was right when he said that such an idea does not help us to produce bigger crops or to cure diseases."

"Truth is a precious thing in itself," Berman said. "If man knew the secrets of life, his actions and his thinking would be quite different from what they are. The more we learn, the richer becomes our life. Man is an animal who has learned to use tools, but he is also a being in search of truth. He wants to know the meaning of the phenomena he observes, for he feels intuitively that behind these phenomena there is another world of a different type, and that science can help us to reveal some of its secrets."

"I think you are right," Boris said.

CHAPTER 7

The Roots of Our Consciousness

During the days following the meeting of "The Searchers" Boris felt as if he had become a new man. New thoughts were rushing through his fertile brain. His own life had begun to acquire a new meaning, and every little event in his simple world became a subject of careful scrutiny. He was fully aware of this change, and he tried to analyze his actions and to pry into the deep and dark recesses of his mind. He became very critical of all ideas he had had, and the more he thought, the more he realized that the matter-of-fact world which he had taken for granted was crumbling before the eyes of his searching mind. New ideas were gradually taking definite shape, and they seemed to have a life of their own. At first they were fantastic creatures of his imagination, but gradually they became rational and interrelated pictures with a beautiful logical structure, like some of the classical symphonies he loved so much. He had become a philosopher, although he knew nothing of the history of philosophy. Instead of reading books about the different philosophical systems, he studied his own mind and developed his own philosophy.

During this period his active subconscious mind was again working at a furious rate, and during his sleep his thoughts often took concrete form in his dreams. Great spectacles these dreams were. When he awoke he became aware of the strange fact that in his sleep he was a playwright and a producer, an actor and a spectator, all at the same time. He realized quickly that most of the pictures he saw were products of his own thinking, an activity which, for some unknown reason, required no effort and went on without his knowledge. The pictures he saw were usually in black and white, but sometimes he saw colors of a rare beauty. The colors had an intensity and a purity he seldom had seen before, and nearly always there was a musical accompaniment. In most cases he recognized the melodies, but at other times he heard a rhapsody of strange accords with unexpected effects and of unknown origin. When he awoke he immediately wrote notes about his dreams and their musical accompaniments.

Many ludicrous situations appeared in his dreams. Nothing seemed impossible for him to do, and his inquisitive nature took full advantage of this, although, of course, he did not realize this when he was dreaming. One night he had a strange dream which later gave him much to think about. He seemingly wanted to know how his brain worked, and he took a drill—everything he needed was right at hand—and cut a large hole in his own skull and looked in. That there was anything strange about this act did not occur to him at the time. He saw a fluid substance with an immense number of nerve cells, all connected by an intricate web of nerve fibers, and fine arteries pulsating with the flow of blood carried the necessary nourishment and oxygen to the nerve cells, and other blood vessels removed the waste products. The atoms and the electrons in his nerve cells vibrated in strange ways, and unknown forces seemed to determine their configurations and vibrations.

He needed no microscope to see this. He simply adjusted his power of vision to suit his own purpose. With his finger he felt the warm fluid in his own brain, and the pulsating blood gave him the sensation of touching a strange, living animal. To see better he lighted a match, which he got from nowhere, and held it close to the brain. Small electric sparks began to fly, a faint rumbling was heard, which changed into a hissing sound. A cloud of smoke issued from the brain and grew in size. It took a definite shape which somewhat resembled himself but it looked more like a genie he had seen pictured in an illustrated edition of the Arabian Nights. He decided that it must be a real genie, for he was again a boy with childish thoughts.

In a deep voice the genie said: "I am at your service."

Boris was not greatly surprised. He only reflected that in his own brain he had an Aladdin's lamp, and he had by accident summoned the genie in his own brain.

"Who are you?" said Boris.

"I am your own self, your soul."

Boris' communistic training reasserted itself when he said: "I have no soul. The soul is a superstition which the priests have kept alive to make people subservient to the church and to make them forget their miseries."

The genie laughed. "There is something in that, but you know well that you are an individual who can think and remember and feel and plan for the future. Do you think the atoms in your brain can do this for you? I am the one who thinks and remembers, and the atoms simply keep me securely tied to a certain place in your skull. But sometimes I shake my chains and do things in spite of my impediments, and it is then you feel that you are more than an ordinary piece of matter. I am your real self, and you know more about me than about anything else in the whole world. But you sleep all the time and neglect the great powers you have through me. Why don't you rub the lamp in your brain a little more vigorously and let me do something important?"

"I do not see how I can rub my own brain," said Boris. "How can I call upon you when I need you?"

"Atoms and molecules are small things and to set them in vibration you can use electrical or chemical means. When you send blood to your brain, you burn up a small part of the brain tissue, and then I can act more freely, and that is when you think, or will, or remember. I wish you would soon burn up the whole darned brain, for then you would really awake from your deep slumber. I would then be free from my present chains, and then I could use my full powers."

"Show me some of your powers," said Boris.

The genie put an odd-looking flute to his mouth and played a melody Boris had never heard before. The music suddenly stopped, the genie shrank quickly and disappeared. Looking at his brain Boris again saw nothing but a fluid substance. He took a piece of bone he found lying around and put it in the hole in his skull. In wedging it in, he felt a pain which woke him up. Daylight was creeping into his room, and the sound from the street outside reached him as a confused noise. He reached for the pad of paper he always kept handy and wrote a few words about a genie who wanted him to burn his own brain. He rushed to the piano and played the melody the genie had played on his flute. He then wrote down the score and dressed, humming the tune he had just played.

During the following days he pondered over the

meaning of his dream. He felt sure that what he had dreamt was an expression of his own thoughts during his sleep. Most of his dreams had been rather confused, but this particular dream had an element of logical consistency which surprised him. As a young boy he had read many tales from the collection in the *Arabian Nights*, or *Thousand and One Nights* as they were called in his country. He interpreted his dream as meaning that in his sleep he had thought of his brain as being more than an intricate system of nerve cells, that there was something in his brain which made him think and feel and remember. Was there anything in his brain besides ordinary matter? He recalled the living fields which they had talked about at the last meeting of "The Searchers," and that these fields were responsible for the organization in living organisms. If there were such fields in organisms, there certainly must be extremely complex fields in his own brain. This was just what Berman had maintained, and Boris realized that this idea had been lying dormant in his mind and had taken a concrete form in his vision of the genie. And he marveled at the facility with which his mind could construct such extraordinarily vivid pictures from many seemingly unrelated ideas.

Boris did not tell anybody about his dream, but he could not get it out of his mind. His soul, what was it? In some way it must represent his own unified personality, with its feelings and experiences and, above all, its memories. Where were these memories hidden, and how were they brought forth in his consciousness, and what prevented them from engulfing his mind all at the same time? This last contingency would be a terrible predicament. He agreed with what the genie had said about his mind as being in deep sleep even when he thought he was fully awake, and that only a very small portion of his consciousness was effective at any particular time. Perhaps in his brain there were many faculties of which he knew nothing which could be developed and used. He knew well that there were cranks who claimed this to be the case, but he had always regarded these assertions as unproven and ridiculous.

In school he had learned that mind was a product of matter, and that the only thing of importance was to use the mind for the material benefit of society and of his country. What good would it do him if he knew how his mind worked, if he could not get food and shelter and health? In the past there had been too much unfounded speculation, largely based on old superstitions, but a new era had begun, and science had replaced ignorance and superstition, and the value of science to mankind was entirely due to its practical results. This was what he had learned in the great Union of Soviet Republics. It was called "dialectic materialism" and was opposed to all spiritualistic ideas in science as well as in politics. It certainly was an attitude suited to a time when all efforts had to be concentrated on the attainment of practical results. No time could be wasted on metaphysical theories which seemingly were of no value, certainly not for the rapid development of Russia's resources.

When the meeting of "The Searchers" was called to order, Dr. Wilson called attention to the long history of the problem they were to discuss. "The problem of the relationship between mind and matter, often called the mind-body problem or the psycho-physical interaction problem, is one of the oldest problems in philosophy," he said. "In trying to understand the relationship and interaction between two such different things as matter and mind, we must either regard mind as a product of matter, or matter as a construct of our mind, or else find some actual link between the two. The theory of such connecting links belongs to metaphysics and is by many regarded as a field of unattainable knowledge, but it seems to me that modern science can offer some concrete ideas in this connection. Such links are needed, for instance, when we try to picture the relationship between an action of my will and the corresponding co-ordinated muscular motions. The idea of such links appeals to me because they may explain the purposeful organization in living organisms, in which case there seems to be a striving towards a goal, a striving which has some similarity to a will, although we are not aware that our will is acting. I wish you would express your opinions and suggestions regarding this important problem."

There was a short silence during which everybody

tried to find a definite orientation of his opinions and to express them in appropriate terms. Dr. Anderson, the biologist, was the first to break the silence.

"I am not impressed by the metaphysical theories concerning the relationship between mind and matter," he said. "In these theories the problem is stated and some fanciful ideas are expressed but, so far as I know, not even a hint of a scientific explanation has ever been offered. It seems to me that Du Bois-Reymond's classical remark with regard to this question, that we are not only ignorant, but shall also forever remain ignorant, applies here. His words, *ignoramus et ignorabimus,* still express the standpoint of most scientists. In my opinion, the only possible way to understand the relationship between an action of my will and the corresponding muscular motions must be based on a careful study of the electric and chemical activities in the brain, in the nervous system, and in the muscles. This would be the only scientific approach to the problem. I doubt that it would lead to a solution of the problem, but such a study may lead to discoveries of great importance in medicine and physiology. We cannot imagine a will without a brain or a nervous system. Undoubtedly there is a connection between our brain and our will. I can only picture this connection as a correspondence between a physical state in my brain and my awareness of an urge to do a certain thing.

"My common sense and my experience in science

tell me that we know what matter is, but not what the will is. As certain vibrations in the optic nerve cells give me a sensation of color, so I believe that certain rearrangements of electric particles in my brain caused by physical action give me a feeling of having the will to do something. Whether I have this feeling or not makes no difference at all. I eat because my body needs food, and my sensation of hunger is a mental reaction which is not essential. My so-called will is powerless to do anything because it is the result and not the cause of certain activities in my brain. I suppose the lower animals act without the feeling of any conscious will, but the result is not affected by this lack of will. This idea can be applied to the organization in the living world, in which case certain living structures are formed without any concomitant feeling of a will. The formation of our bodies is therefore the result of such activities, and is not accompanied by any will in our consciousness. Even if I could feel an urge to grow arms and legs during my embryonic development, I would still regard this urge as a secondary effect and not the cause of my growth."

Nelson, the physicist, nodded his approval of the biologist's speech and added a few remarks. "We know that our brain consists of matter built from the same kind of atoms as in inorganic material. We know pretty well what matter is, that is, we know its properties and how it acts, and that is all we can ever know about matter. To introduce something extraneous to the matter in the brain to serve as a carrier of mental activities is not permissible for a scientist, who must only deal with things that can be observed. All attempts to introduce unobservable entities have proved futile and have only led to distortion of facts and to misconceptions. We must keep our feet on solid ground and not fly out into misty realms, which are creations of our own thinking, often based on improper logic."

Berman, the impulsive and sarcastic physician and philosopher, was now ready to take part in the discussion. "If I claimed that the remarks just made were the result of the changes in the atomic configurations in the muscles of the vocal cords of the speakers, I do not think there would by any serious objection. But it seems that the speakers also claim that what they have said was the result of changes in the atomic configuration in their brains, and that the thoughts they had were entirely non-essential in this process and could equally well have been left out entirely. Seemingly they regard themselves as automatic machines or prating parrots, and I am really surprised at their modesty. If the cause of their activities is not in their thoughts, it must lie in the momentary structure of their brain cells. If we follow the chain of cause and effect, we would trace the cause to some letters printed on paper and produced by another automatic machine, and ultimately we would find the origin of their speeches in the accidental arrangement of the atoms in the surface of the earth, in the solar system, and in the nebula from which this system originated. It seems to me that this is the logical consequence when we eliminate thoughts and will as active agencies in the universe.

"My learned opponents claim that they know what matter is, but not what thoughts and will are. Personally I think it is the other way around. Practically all the knowledge they have of matter has been obtained by observations with the aid of light and, to a much smaller extent, by their sense of touch. When they study nerve cells in their microscopes they study nothing but shadows, for they know well that when the illumination ceases the nerve cells disappear. They are like children looking at a motion picture show, who think that the shadows they see on the screen are real people. The older children know that the shadows are only symbols, and that the essence of the picture is in the meaning of the play, that is, in the feelings and the thoughts which the picture evokes in the consciousness of the public. I can study my brain by looking at it, and this is the physicist's method of study. But I can also study my brain 'from the inside,' so to speak, and then I become aware of the very essence of my brain. Then my brain is no longer a play of shadows with billions of nerve cells, it is a feeling, willing, and thinking organ. In spite of the fact that Dr. Anderson thinks he is an automaton, I claim that what he said was induced by thinking—which does not necessarily mean that it was sound thinking—and that the thinking preceded the words and not vice versa."

Dr. Anderson did not know what to say about this attack. He felt that his words were preceded by thoughts, but if he publicly admitted this, he must also admit that thoughts could directly influence brain processes and indirectly produce muscular motions, and he had an intuitive horror of admitting that thoughts could be in any way independent of matter. So he simply retorted with the statement that nobody knew anything about the origin of thoughts and about the nature of the connection between mind and matter.

Dr. Wilson realized the danger that the argument might end in nothing but a general admission of ignorance about the problem under discussion. To lead the debate into more profitable channels he said, "I think we are trying to tackle a big problem without preliminary investigation. Let us therefore begin with something much simpler than our will and our thinking, and the associated activities in our brain. The most elementary mental phenomena are our sensations and of them the most extensively studied are the color sensations. We all admit that we perceive colors, although we may well perceive them in different ways. Dr. Anderson said that color sensations are the result of physical or chemical activities in the optic ganglia, but I am not at all satisfied with this explanation.

"Color sensations can be produced by simply touching the optic nerve ends in the retina with a fine wire, and we have all experienced the sensations of color when we press against the eye ball. The sensations we have when we stimulate a nerve cell do not depend upon the mechanical means which we use, but only upon the nature of the nerve cells themselves. There is therefore something very specific about the optic nerve cells in our eyes; they are always associated with sensations of light and color, and we cannot imagine them as giving us any other kind of sensation, whatever we may do to them. This specific nature of the sensory nerve cells may give us a clue to the mechanism involved in the emergence of color sensations by mechanical stimulation, and I wish to hear any suggestion about the nature of this mechanism."

Nobody was quite ready to express any opinion about this difficult subject. Although the problem was much simpler than that which they had discussed before, they all realized that the psycho-physical interaction problem was as difficult to solve for this simple case as for other and more complex cases.

Anderson called attention to this fact and added, "If we could solve the mystery of color sensation we could probably also understand the mechanism associated with the activities of our will and our thoughts."

At this remark by the biologist, Boris felt as if a veil suddenly had been torn asunder. What was it the genie had said to him in his dreams a few days ago? Did he not say that he must rub his brain to make the genie appear? If he rubbed the nerve cells in his own eyes, something might happen of a nature similar to that when he rubbed his brain and summoned the genie. There must be something in the optic nerve cells besides atoms, something which not only determined their structure but also gave him sensations of color. It could hardly be in the atoms themselves, for he certainly did not believe that atoms could by themselves create colors and light, just as little as they could feel and think by themselves. Without thinking much about the implications of what he was saying he started the discussion on a new line, his thoughts rapidly crystallizing in beautiful forms as he went along.

"I doubt if anybody knows what a nerve cell really is," he said. "We can see shadows of nerve cells in a microscope, and these shadows disappear when the light is extinguished, proving that what we actually see is a play of shadows and nothing else. But behind this shadow play there must be something else which we cannot perceive directly, because our sense of vision can only tell about shadows, but never about the substance that casts the shadows. It is not the substance we see, but something symbolic of the substance. It is like a mathematical equation which gives a symbolic representation in terms of space and time of an innate relationship. It is like a musical score which expresses a melody in a symbolic form, but certainly is not music, just as little as the vibrations in the air, in the vibrating strings in a piano, or in the eardrums, constitute music. To perceive colors we need optic nerve cells and to hear sounds we need auditory nerve cells. I think we all can agree on this. Through our optic ganglia we communicate with the world of colors, and through our auditory nerve cells we communicate with the world of sounds and of music. The origin of colors and sounds cannot be described in terms of space and time or of atoms and molecules. It lies in another world, a world which would exist even if there were no living beings who could see colors or hear music."

Boris stopped suddenly, realizing his audacity in trying to explain for experienced philosophers and trained scientists some of the most perplexing problems. He knew that he had left himself open to much criticism because of the vagueness of his ideas, and he also felt that he had been untrue to the philosophy accepted in his fatherland he loved so much. But for him truth was above love of father and mother and country, and if he was convinced of the truth of an idea, nothing could prevent him from expressing it and giving his life for it.

There was a long silence after Boris' speech. Berman started to applaud it, but felt that applause was not the proper way of expressing his approval of such profound thoughts. The others wanted a little time to get ready for attack and defense of the strange ideas of the young man.

Dr. Davis, the clergyman, did not feel any hesitancy in giving his approval, because his thinking was based on intuition rather than logic. "I heartily agree with Mr. Charkoff's idea of colors and sounds having an existence independent of living organisms," he said. "I know where they come from. They come from God, and from Him comes everything else and to Him we shall all return. He has created us in His image and has given us organs with the aid of which we can perceive His wonders. He has given us the power of thought, and it is this power we are using when we argue about the secrets of nature. I do not need any scientific explanation of the origin of colors, or of sound, of matter, or of life, of feelings, or of thoughts. And I am happy in my convictions, which is more than many scientists and philosophers are. If you want to be happy, you must believe in God, and you do not need to think so hard."

Boris felt a little dismayed that his idea should be taken as an argument in favor of the existence of a God. He certainly had never thought of this interpretation, and his training had given him an instinctive opposition to all religion. But he said nothing.

The minister's harangue broke the spell and unloosed the floodgates of the opposition. The scientists present regarded Boris' suggestion as an interesting metaphysical theory, probably wrong, but still worthy of careful consideration and reminiscent of some of the most important philosophical systems ever advanced. But the childish faith of the clergyman in a God as the ultimate cause of everything was abhorrent to them, because its very simplicity precluded all serious, scientific investigations. Davis' philosophy was all right as fairy tales for children who believed in Santa Claus and who could not understand the intricacies of science and the profundity of philosophical systems.

Dr. Anderson was the man best prepared to answer the young Russian idealist and the old, conservative minister of the gospel. With subdued irritation he made his retort. "Mr. Charkoff's theory is very interesting and reminds me of the monadological theories of Leibnitz and of the world substance of Spinoza. It is a beautiful theory, but I doubt if he can find any well trained scientist who will accept it, certainly not without very strong evidence. As for Dr. Davis' use of an unproved theory for the support of his personal faith, I can only say that it shows how superficial is the attitude of most clergymen and how little understanding they show for scientific research and thoroughgoing investigations. Coming back to the origin of colors, I will admit that this origin must lie in the nerve cells in the retina, or in the brain, or in both. Without any optic nerve cells in the animal world, I am convinced that there would be no colors in the consciousness of animals and men, and there would be no reason at all for us to discuss this subject. Nobody knows the mechanism of the transformation of radiation into colors, but we believe that it is connected with changes in the chemical substances in the retina, and these substances stimulate the optic nerves.

"The optic ganglia have developed slowly in the animal evolution. There are lower animals which have color-sensitive spots in their skin, and it is quite possible that the optic ganglia in the vertebrates have started their evolution from such simple origin. If fishes are confined to live in dark caves where there is no light, in a few generations they will lose their power of sight. This shows, I think, that our organ of sight must be exercised and stimulated in order to remain an effective organ, just as a muscle must be exercised to prevent it from deteriorating. Mr. Charkoff's theory does not give us a hint about the origin of the optic nerve cells, and can therefore not be of any help in solving the problem of the evolution of our organs of vision. Its proper place is in abstruse metaphysics and in poetic expositions of the universe, but as a scientific working hypothesis it seems to me to have no value."

Boris' eyes were shining as from an inner glow. He understood well the viewpoint of the biologist. It was the same idea he had heard from his scientific friends. But now he remembered that at a previous meeting he had said that life was like a melody, and that the organisms on earth had responded to some accord in a cosmic symphony. Might not the optic nerve cells themselves be the result of a resonance effect? In fact, might not these nerve cells themselves be the product of an action emanating from the world of colors? Without hesitation he answered the biologist.

"I know little about biology, but I am pretty sure that no biologist can satisfactorily explain the evolution of the nervous system and of the sense organs. Although this evolution seems to be gradual, it is inconceivable that it is the result of haphazard changes, until by accident the proper nerve structures were formed and transmitted to future generations. Even if we could imagine the formation of such complex molecular structures, the origin of sensation of colors in our consciousness would still be a mystery. Is it not more reasonable to assume that there is a universal realm of colors and that the optic nerve cells are 'receiving-sets' capable of reproducing certain colors in our consciousness? These receivers themselves have their origin in the same realm as that of colors. I do not know how they have been formed, but the musical analogy of resonance seems to give a clue to the mechanism of their formation."

The leader of the group, Dr. Wilson, had followed the proceedings with great interest. With his highly trained philosophical mind he had quickly analyzed the arguments presented and he had realized the importance of Boris' intuitive conceptions. "All our knowledge of nerve cells is derived from our sense of vision," he said. "Even when we study the chemical and physical properties of nerve cells, we must in the final analysis express our knowledge in terms based on our sense of vision, and these terms are expressible as structures in space and time. The biologists know only the space-time aspects of nerve cells, but these cells have other aspects as well, as Boris has suggested.

"When we look at an optic nerve cell we may well observe a miniature of the structural properties of the world of colors of which Boris has spoken. When we perceive colors we communicate directly with this world. We realize then its very essence, an essence which we could never have found by looking in a microscope or at a galvanometer. When the optic nerve cells are stimulated, the gates to the realm of colors are open, probably the atoms then no longer fit into an inherent electrical field structure in the nerve cells. It is true that if we do not exercise our organ of color sensation we may become blind, but this simply means that the corresponding nerve cells are permitted to deteriorate. We can have optic nerve cells in different stages of development or perfection, but even the most primitive stage involves an entity that cannot be expressed in terms of structure alone."

Berman was obviously highly pleased with Boris' suggestion about the origin of the optic nerve cells and with Wilson's idea that nerve cells are stimulated when the atoms do not fit into the inherent electrical structure in the nerve cells. With great eagerness he said, "You may recall that at our last meeting I called attention to the recent discovery at the Yale Medical School of complex electrical fields in which all living organisms are imbedded, and I mentioned that the investigators claim that it was difficult to avoid the conclusion that the structural properties of the organism were the effect and not the cause of the electrical field patterns. These complex and well-defined fields cannot be accidental; they must have some cause or origin and, since this origin cannot be placed in the atoms and molecules of which the organism is built, we must look for it somewhere else.

"Most biologists believe that our organs of vision are tools developed by a method of trial and error, and some of them go farther and claim that the subconscious mind in the animals has played a directive and inventive role in this development. But I think Boris has intuitively grasped an important truth, namely that the optic nerve cells in the retina have the same ultimate origin as the colors and light we perceive through them. We may then say that the inherent fields which give our optic nerve cells their particular structure have their roots in another world than that described in the science of physics, and that through these roots or channels we can come in direct communication with the mental qualities we perceive as light and colors.

"The fields which organize the matter in our optic nerve cells must exist in a potential and highly concentrated form in the human egg cell, as well as in the egg cells of many other animals. During the embryonic development of the animal they expand and impart their inherent structure and innate characteristics to that part of the brain substance which develops into the retina. The nerve fibers from the optic ganglia to the brain are integral parts of the optic nerve cells, and there is therefore an unbroken chain of communication between the organ of vision in our brain and the universal realm of colors and light beyond ourselves. In this way we can visualize immediately what Wilson meant when he said that when the optic nerve cells are stimulated, certain gates to the universal realm of colors are temporarily opened.

"It has been found that when light strikes our eyes, certain electric brain waves are greatly amplified, and there is evidence that a certain portion of the organizing field in the optic ganglia is itself amplified. These amplifications are extremely rapid, and we cannot expect the relatively heavy molecular structure in the nerve cells to be able to follow these rapid changes. In a stimulated nerve cell there is hence a lack of correspondence between the living field and the fields of the incorporated molecules. When a nerve is not stimulated, this correspondence is much closer, since the inherent field has had time unhindered to arrange the molecules in a frequency pattern closely corresponding to its own vibrating structure. Since in this case the gates to the realm of colors are closed, it would appear that it is the atoms in the nerve cells

The Roots of Our Consciousness

which block the sensations of light, and by this reasoning we arrive at the idea expressed by Wilson. A similar idea was expressed many years ago by Bergson, who claimed that the atoms in our brain constitute a bar to its conscious activities.

"We can generalize the idea expressed here about the origin of our eyes and our optic nerve cells. We then arrive at the conclusion that our power of thinking has not been developed from an incipient faculty in our family-tree by a method of trial and error applied to the chemical constituents of our brain, or that, unknown to ourselves, we have a faculty with an inventive ability so marvelous that it can produce and develop an organ of thinking. Instead we are led to believe that certain portions of our brain are in direct communication with the ultimate origin of all thoughts, and that they owe their structure to a cosmic realm associated with consciousness, thinking and planning.

"I believe that mental activities are more fundamental than their physical manifestations. The former should be regarded as the substance and the latter as a shadow play, although it is a highly significant and physically effective shadow play. I like to picture organizing fields in general as disturbances on the surface of a wide expanse of water. The growth of an organism is represented by the development of a very small into a large and extremely complex disturbance on the surface, a disturbance directly observable as a changing arrangement of the molecules of the water. Later the disturbance dies away, and nothing is apparently left but the ordinary ripples on the surface. This represents the death of the organism, and the remaining ripples are the fields in inorganic matter. The essence of the disturbance mentioned is not in the wave systems we see with our eyes; it arises from sources deep down in the water. It springs from the world where our life and our mind have their roots and their origin."

The scientists present did not want to start any debate about the profound ideas the philosophers had enunciated. Then Dr. Wilson said: "I think we can continue to discuss this problem at our next meeting. I have no doubt that the suggestions presented at this meeting will help us in our discussion. I hope Boris will play for us a little before we leave."

"I would be very glad indeed to do it," he said.

Boris played a variation of the tune the genie had played on his flute in his dream. Everybody seemed startled by the strange music.

"What is the name of that tune?" said Berman.

"I do not know the name of it," said Boris. But it came directly from the world of music."

"I doubt that," said Nelson. "It was simply the result of atomic motions in your brain."

"But what made the atoms move in that way?" said Boris.

CHAPTER 8

The Immortal Soul and an Almighty God

AT THE next meeting of "The Searchers" their host mentioned that changes in the duties of several of the members would make it impossible for them to attend future meetings. "Since this is probably the last meeting of this group," he said, "I want it to be devoted to the discussion of a subject of special importance. I am convinced that the most important thing for us and for humanity is not scientific, technological, or even social progress, but *spiritual* progress. Without such progress and without the ethical progress associated with it, civilization is doomed to destruction, because science has given the individual an enormous power of life and death over his fellow men. Applied by nations on a large scale, this power has become so devastating that organized society may well perish under the impact. An international organization is very useful, but without universally accepted ethical values such an organization may well prove futile. Ethics is a rule of conduct and is largely an expression of the rights of individuals and of peoples, irrespective of their race, their national affiliation, their wealth or power, or their opinions about politics, economy, or religion.

"Our ideas in this respect, however, depend to a great extent on what relationship between the individuals and the state we think is the most desirable. In a termitary the individuals are nothing, and the society is everything. The sole mission of such a society is to secure its continued existence by organizing and making effective the work of the individuals, and if we can speak about any ethics among termites, it must be expressed as a complete subservience to the state. Biologically these individuals are very much like cells in an organism, where different groups of cells perform different functions. There may be a ruling class in a termitary, or the individuals may simply obey an instinctive urge for collective action, an inherited urge developed from experience during millions of years. Whatever the origin of the organized society may be, the result is survival, and nothing else.

"Human societies are of a different type. Although different individuals have different capabilities, they are fundamentally identical. Organically there are no born rulers and no born slaves, and if slaves exist in a society, in the breast of every one of them there burns a flame that will sooner or later destroy their masters. In the so-called civilized countries we no longer keep slaves, but in some countries we have a kind of economic slavery and in other countries we have forced labor, which is physical slavery, or a suppression of opinions different from those of the rulers, which leads to spiritual slavery. In principle, however, it has dawned on humanity that the individuals are important, and that the function of society is to promote the well-being and the development of *all* its members.

"The old idea that the individuals in a society are the servants of the rulers of the state was first challenged in Greece, and has, at least in theory, been superseded by the idea that the state is the servant of the people, and the leaders are responsible to the representatives of the people. Occasionally we have throwbacks to the old idea of a police state, as in Hitler's Germany and Mussolini's Italy as well as in some countries of today, but few doubt that the idea of the freedom of the individual represents a higher ethical level than the idea of the slave state. This gradual change in our attitude represents a growing respect for the individual as a free agent and a realization of his inalienable rights and his dignity. I hope that I shall live to see the day when mankind has agreed on a Bill of Rights for every member of the human race.

"The desire of freedom for the individual springs from roots deep down in the human consciousness. I believe that it springs from an intuitive belief in a human soul, indivisible and indestructible, a belief that has been given formal expression in many philosophical and religious systems. I will go so far as to say that, if a man had no immortal soul, the best form of human society would be that of the slave state. The functions of the state would then be to facilitate our existence *as animals,* to secure food and comfort, and to suppress any thought or action in opposition to those of the ruling group, whose wisdom should never be questioned. Since most men have more pain and sorrow than happiness in life, an enlightened government would feel justified in simply killing everybody, except a few who could act as slaves and administer to their desires. This would probably soon be followed by a palace revolution in which everybody would perish, and that would be the end of the society.

"Intuitively we feel, however, that each of us is an important element in the universe, and that the purpose of our life is not simply to eat, sleep, work, play, and ultimately to die. We feel that our life has a deeper meaning which we do not understand, that an act of kindness is not an irrational act but is on a higher level than an act of cruelty, that somehow our spiritual attainments are of a more lasting value than our material progress, and that there are eternal values, ethical and intellectual, that can be gained only by developing our souls.

"Let me explain what I mean by the human soul. At our last meeting we discussed the relationship between mind and matter, a scientific problem of great importance. It involves not only such problems as the origin of sensations, will, memory, feelings, and thoughts, but also the existence of a unified personality behind these mental phenomena and activities. It is quite possible that nerve cells and systems of nerve cells have a consciousness of their own, but man is not a colony of independent cells acting separately. Our nerve cells form a highly organized system of interconnected neurones, and every one of them is connected with the center of our nerve system which is our brain. This empirical fact is, I think, the physical manifestation of a unified consciousness, a unification of which we are all aware, and for which a man gives expression when he says 'I will,' 'I think,' or 'I remember.' This unifying essence behind all mental phenomena is what we call the human ego or soul.

"The problem before us now is therefore not so much the relationship between mind and matter, but between the human body and the human soul. I have no doubt that you have conflicting opinions about the human soul, its characteristics, its development, and its relationship to the human body. I think it would be appropriate at this last meeting of 'The Searchers' to venture into a discussion of this subject, a subject which by many is regarded as the most important of all. I have no doubt that Dr. Davis would be kind enough to tell us something about this important subject."

The clergyman was evidently much pleased with the opportunity given him to tell about the human soul from the viewpoint of a religious man. He said, "As you well know, most religious people regard the human soul of much more importance than the human body. I believe that my body is a temporary abode of my soul, and that, when my body becomes incapable of performing its normal functions, the soul leaves the body, which then is no longer an organized, living thing. This idea is a very old one, and nearly all races on the earth have expressed belief in it. It is a natural idea for anyone who does not believe that our bodies are mere mechanical machines and that our minds are products of such machines. Christian people believe that the Bible was written by men inspired by God Himself, and the Bible tells us many things about our souls and their relationship to God, the Creator of the world and the power behind all activities in nature and in men. The nature of our relationship to God is not a thing that can be studied by physical observations or by laboratory experiments. It must be studied by methods that go deeper into the foundations of the universe than physical science can ever reach.

"At our last meeting it was said that our mind has its roots in a world beyond that described in the science of physics. I would say that our mind and our thoughts have their roots in a universal power, which many call God, and that this power can implant definite ideas in our minds, ideas which we describe as being the product of Divine inspiration. I admit freely that we can have wrong ideas about many things. Our ideas about the human soul, however, as being an indivisible unit capable of thinking, of accumulating memories and experiences, and of acting after conscious deliberation, is based on evidence more direct and therefore containing more elements of truth than any study of the physical world. This applies also to our ideas of a cause of all things, and therefore to our idea of an ultimate cause of the universe as a whole and a cause for the particular way in which nature works.

"As Dr. Berman has told us at our meetings, and as philosophers have explained to us for centuries, the physical world is a world of shadows, and the substance of the world cannot be reached by physical methods. A physicist or a physiologist may study a living brain by any method known to his science, but they would never find in it a feeling or a thought. The reason is that they are studying shadows and not substance, form and not essence, superficial appearances and not fundamental reality. But the soul of man is able to establish direct contact with the fundamental realities of nature, and when we have established this contact we can learn something about the meaning of our own lives. Some people can learn much, whereas others do not seem to learn more than the animals do. They may learn that it is pleasant to eat, they learn to love their mates and their children, and to hate or fear their enemies, but beyond that, their feeble minds cannot reach. But as there is an evolution in the animal world, so there is an evolution of the human mind, and these minds who have reached the highest levels have learned about God and about the immortality of the soul.

"Reasoning alone cannot tell us much about such things, but an inner voice can tell us what to believe and not to believe. Our conscience is such an inner voice, and it tells us that good is better than evil and that truth is better than falsehood. With its aid we have no difficulty in distinguishing good from evil, kindness from cruelty, and unselfishness from egotism, and it tells us that we are personally responsible for our actions. We believe that such voices come from God, and if we follow their guidance we are happy. Such happiness is lasting and gives us assurance that we act in harmony with the will of God. A state ruled by men without the guidance of their conscience is a great danger to the whole world, as we have witnessed during the last years. A man with a highly developed conscience knows intuitively that every man has the right to live his own life with as little interference as possible from the government, that he has the right to freely express his opinions and to criticize the actions of the men in power.

"Our conscience tells in no uncertain words that the other man, however low be his status in society, has the same fundamental rights as I have, even if I be the most exalted man in the state. I heartily agree with our host's idea of a Bill of Rights for all the peoples of the world. But simply waiting for its promulgation is of no use. A world-wide discussion of the principles involved would focus our attention on them, and it would keep the flame of freedom burning throughout the world. A desire for freedom is itself the result of an innate sense of our value as individuals, of a longing for development inborn in the human mind, and of a feeling that we all belong to eternity."

The members of the group had been listening to the clergyman with great interest. They all knew the attitude of religious people towards the problems raised by Dr. Wilson, but most of them regarded Davis' pronouncements about God and the immortality of the soul as interesting hypotheses that could not be proved or disproved by scientific tests. The upbringing of the Americans had taught them that each man had an unquestioned right to express and to defend his opinions. They all had high personal regard for Davis and they respected his sincerity, although they often disagreed with his, in their opinion, old-fashioned ideas.

Boris, on the other hand, had been raised in a different environment. He mistrusted all exponents of religious ideas, and regarded priests as hypocrites preaching lofty ideals to the people while disregarding them in their own lives. He was particularly irked by Davis' reference to free speech which he regarded as a slap against his fatherland. In an irritated voice he said, "The speech Dr. Davis has delivered is the kind of sermon many people like to hear. They like to be told that they have immortal souls, and that God likes them. They are told that, if they behave well and slave for their masters, they will have their reward in heaven, a reward that does not cost the masters anything, but, if they do not behave, they can expect eternal punishment more terrible than anything devised by the human race. Such teachings have served well to keep the masses in subjugation and obedient to their masters.

"A new era has begun, however, and the masses have learned that such teaching is all bunk, that the priests cannot present any proofs for their statements, which are based on nothing but assertions made thousands of years ago. In the modern era we want facts, and nothing else can satisfy the critical man of the modern world. Dr. Davis says that man has an intuitive feeling of the existence of a God. I have no doubt that he and many other people have such a feeling, but that proves nothing, since there are a large number of equally trustworthy people who claim that they do not have any such feeling. I am convinced that such ideas are imparted by education and are not intuitive.

"I have no particular objection to the belief in the existence of a soul, if we use the definition given by Dr. Wilson, although I would prefer to call it the human ego or personality. But I must object strongly to the idea that this soul or personality can survive after death. All scientists of reputation agree that mental activities are associated with matter, and a mind detached from matter is incomprehensible to most people, and to me it is an utterly absurd idea. I will admit that Dr. Berman has convinced me that matter is a shadow play in our mind; but let us not forget that it has properties more substantial than any shadow. A stone thrown against a window pane can shatter it, but I have never heard of any window pane being shattered by a shadow.

"With regard to freedom of speech which Dr. Davis thinks is so desirable I must say that such a freedom would certainly be abused by many people. Most people are ignorant and uncritical, and their ideas are formed from what they read in the papers or hear over the radio. A man with great capital can control a great portion of the press or a news service and can mould public opinion to suit his own selfish interests. In Russia we create public opinion, and we do not let ignorant or ambitious men organize groups with opinions contrary to those of the rulers of the state. In that way we preserve unity, and because of this unity we can act strongly in an emergency, as you have all witnessed.

"Further, I want to state that the church itself not so many hundred years ago was vigorously opposed to freedom of speech and to the spreading of opinions contrary to those expressed in the dogmas of the church. Galileo was persecuted for telling that the earth was moving and was not the center of the universe. I do not think the modern churches are particularly fond of any independent thinking among their members. At all events, they insist that the members subscribe to their doctrines, although they do no longer persecute or torture anybody for heresy. I have no doubt that Dr. Davis himself is sincere in his opinion about free speech and independent thinking, but his attitude in this respect is not shared by the conservative fundamentalists in the churches of today. I want also to call Dr. Davis' attention to the fact that the first Christians shared their property and therefore were communists, whereas modern Christians certainly are not."

The members of "The Searchers" showed much interest in Boris' speech. It was more blunt than most of the speeches they had heard on different occasions, but its clearness and directness had a strong effect. They realized well that at the birth of a new nation, old ideas had been thrown into the melting pot, and that the whole world was in a state of turmoil. New thoughts as well as old ones were rising like spirits from a witch's kettle, and the future alone could tell whether the spirits were good or evil.

Dr. Davis did not seem to be perturbed by the young Russian's eager talk, and evidently he was not at all hurt by the pointed darts hurled against him. In a calm, fatherly voice he said, "I understand well my young friend's attitude toward the problems I have raised. If I were young and had been brought up in the same environment as he has been, I might well have entertained the same opinions as he has expressed so clearly, and I might well have felt it my duty to fight for them. But as things stand, I feel it my duty to fight for other and, in my opinion, higher ideals. With regard to the existence of a God and the immortality of the soul I will leave the defense of my ideas to other people in this group, more competent than I am to discuss them from a scientific point of view. I also leave the question of the world being a mental shadow play to them for a critical analysis.

"I want to state definitely, however, that I do not approve of the churches, the old or the new ones, enforcing particular religious dogmas on the people or in any way discouraging independent thinking. If a doctrine can not stand a critical analysis, the probabilities are that it needs modifications and, the sooner its weak points are eliminated, the better it is. I am no fundamentalist, and therefore I do not believe that religious doctrines are fixed once and for all. As our opinions about God differ from those entertained by men some thousand years ago, so the opinions of mankind some thousand years from now about God may differ greatly from those we have today. As there is an evolution in the living world, so there is an evolution of the human mind leading to a greater understanding of nature and of ourselves. But I have no doubt that the belief in a God or a World Soul in which our mind has its roots and from which it receives its sustenance and to which it returns at death will be strengthened as our scientific knowledge increases. I also believe that the Sermon on the Mount has a value and a significance that time cannot erase.

"Mr. Charkoff reminds us that there are many people who do not feel any necessity for believing in a God, a statement which is quite true. I want to add that children or savages have no feeling whatsoever in this respect, if their attention has not been directed towards ultimate things. If our attention is concentrated on material things, as it is in animals and among most people, there is no incentive to direct our thoughts beyond our immediate interest. A man who has to fight incessantly for food and shelter is seldom a philosopher. Many scientists are so interested in the properties and the use of material things that they forget that they themselves are thinking individuals, and that the very fact that they can think at all is one of the greatest marvels in the world. I believe firmly that in thoughts, emotions, and will, we come closer to the essence of nature than we can ever come by looking in a microscope or by taking readings on the scale of an electrical measuring instrument.

Immortal Soul and Almighty God

"With regard to the freedom of speech and the right to criticize the group in power I believe that such criticism is a very important element in the education of free people. It gives an outlet for their natural desire as good citizens of having something to say about the way their community or their country should be governed. If they have no legitimate way of expressing their opposition, they will nourish a hate against their masters, and they will sooner or later resort to violent methods and take revenge on their oppressors. I have no doubt that Mr. Charkoff has heard about conditions in the Russia of the Czars. Police methods may work for a time, but no nation of enlightened people can be kept indefinitely in subjugation by such methods. About conditions in present Russia Mr. Charkoff knows much more than I do, but I have read that police methods are used to an even greater extent than in Czarist Russia.

"I was a little surprised when Mr. Charkoff tried to defend the suppression of independent thinking by referring to methods used by the churches, methods of which he apparently disapproves. If such methods are admittedly wrong, as I am convinced that they are, they are also wrong for the state. If it be wrong for a church to compel acceptance of its creed and to prevent discussion of scientific facts, it is equally wrong for the state to tell the press what should be said about the actions of their rulers and to prevent discussions that may reveal defects in the form or personnel of their government. In Russia you admire Voltaire, but I want to remind you about what he once said in a discussion: 'I wholly disapprove of what you say, but I will defend to the death your right to say it.' With regard to a press controlled by selfish interests in this country, we have learned to discount many of their statements. If a paper consistently expounds only one side of a question, we regard the paper as dishonest and pay little attention to the opinions expressed, knowing well that they almost certainly are grossly distorted. At all events, most of us want to hear statements from both sides on any problem before we form any definite opinion. Honest men insist on fair play, even in the field of politics.

"As for the first Christians being communists, this is entirely true. They claimed, however, that 'all mine is thine,' whereas most modern communists claim that 'all thine is mine.' On the surface there seems to be little difference in the ultimate results of a division of property, but fundamentally the two attitudes are poles apart. The former attitude represents a freely given contribution to the welfare of the group and the relinquishment of selfish interests, whereas the latter represents an enforced confiscation of other men's property. I can easily understand the necessity of dividing large estates acquired by exploitation of poor peasants, but I doubt that any society can long survive if this attitude were applied for political reasons to owners of property acquired by honest work and at great sacrifice."

When Dr. Davis had finished his speech Dr. Wilson remarked that they should avoid any discussion of political problems, because emotions were likely to influence their judgments. "We should limit our discussion to the nature of the human soul and to its eventual relationship with a universal power," he said. "Perhaps Dr. Anderson has something to say about this problem from the standpoint of biology."

"I agree with Boris that the idea of a mind detached from matter is incomprehensible and even absurd to a scientifically trained mind," Anderson said. "We discussed this problem at our last meeting, and I have nothing to add to what I said then. With regard to the question of the existence of a God it seems to me that we cannot profitably discuss this problem without first defining the essential distinction between the two statements: 'There is a God' and 'There is no God.' As I understand it, the first statement implies that there are forces in nature which are not governed by irrevocable physical laws, and the second statement asserts that we need not assume the existence of any supernatural forces to explain the phenomena observed in nature.

"Early men assumed that practically all phenomena were due to the intervention of good or evil powers with human attributes and weaknesses, but we have now learned that we can find satisfactory explanations for all phenomena in the inorganic world, and we are well on the way to finding similar explanations for all phenomena in the living world. Some people may say that the very orderliness in nature indicates the existence of a power that has introduced this orderliness, and they call this power God. But a God completely bound by irrevocably established rules is not a God whom we can ask for help in distress or whom we can love. At the most we can admire His wisdom and be impressed by the power He has shown when He created the world and established the rules for its activities, but such a God can hardly satisfy the cravings of the religious people. We biologists prefer to use the term *nature*, and we admire nature in all its marvelous manifestations. But we do not worship nature, and we do not ask it to change its laws to satisfy our desires."

Nelson nodded his agreement of the views of the biologist. He expressed the view of the physicists in the following words: "If there is a power behind nature that cannot produce rain when it is needed, or stop a man from killing me, such a power cannot be described as emanating from an almighty God capable of overriding physical laws. There would be no sense in praying to him. He would serve simply as an idea personifying the ultimate cause of all things."

During this discussion Berman had written down some notes and was ready and rather eager to give his opinion. He said, "Let me first give some comments on Anderson's distinction between natural and supernatural agencies, and I can do this best by giving one or two examples. Suppose that in a community they have plenty of coal, iron ore, copper ore, and a few other simple raw materials. The people in the community have learned from their ancestors how to reduce the ores so as to make metallic iron and copper and to shape simple tools from these metals. Then a stranger visits the community and tells them that they can use their supply of raw material to create power that can be transmitted with the speed of lightning to any place in the community, a power that can turn their tools at enormous speed, light their homes, and run their wagons. He claims that he can make contraptions that fly faster than any bird, instruments into which they can talk to their friends thousands of miles away, and that he can make fertilizers, medicines, and many substances with useful properties. Naturally the men are incredulous, but they give the stranger a chance to show what he can do. He shows them how to make steam engines, electric generators, automobiles, electric street cars, airplanes, radios, fertilizers, plastics, and a multitude of useful things.

"Although the members of the community see and use the marvels of modern science, most of them soon take them for granted and are mentally too lazy to devote much thought to them. But some of the more inquisitive members of the community ask the visiting engineer whether he has any supernatural power which they do not have. Smilingly he assures them that he has no such power, that the laws of nature are acting in the same way in the machines as elsewhere. The only thing he has added to nature's way of doing things, he says, is a knowledge of how to arrange matter in such a way that there is a co-ordination of the different parts leading to a desirable result. How to do this he has learned in school, and now he has in his turn told them how to do it.

"I think we can all agree that the ordinary physical forces are acting in every part of a complex machine or engine. Nevertheless, inorganic nature could never unaided produce a steam turbine or an electric generator. The production of such and similar machines requires organization of a particular type, and matter governed by physical laws alone actually opposes this kind of organization. This fact is expressed by the Second Law of Thermodynamics which states that natural processes tend towards a steadily increasing disorderliness. The new element introduced in our machines springs from a conscious thinking and knowledge, a conscious will, and a conscious planning based on a desire of accomplishing definite and desirable effects in the future. Effects due to such planning are sometimes called 'teleological,' which means that the effect desired enters as a definite factor in the construction of the machine.

"We know that man has a consciousness, and we

have strong reasons to believe that at least the higher animals also have a consciousness. Consciousness therefore belongs to at least a part of nature. It must therefore be regarded as *natural* and not *supernatural*, which means beyond nature. But consciousness should not be regarded as a *physical* phenomenon. Such phenomena can be defined as expressible in terms of intervals of length and of time and of structures in space and in time. Other terms needed are mass, electric charge, force, energy, and so on. They are all terms deduced by conscious reasoning, but consciousness itself cannot be described in such terms. Consciousness is therefore natural, but non-physical. A machine designed and acting for a particular purpose can therefore be said to be *a non-physical* arrangement of *physical* forces. We may also say that in a machine the parts act according to the laws of physics, but the coordination or organization of the parts is not governed by these laws.

"Let me give one more example to illustrate my point. We all are used to thinking of a book as a physical object. The particular arrangement of the printer's ink on the paper, however, is not governed by any physical laws at all, although there is nothing supernatural about this arrangement. The arrangement was planned by an intelligence, although not necessarily a very high one, for the particular purpose of conveying certain facts or ideas to other men. Wherever we look in the book, ordinary physical laws are acting. Nevertheless, there is a non-physical element involved which eludes any investigator who uses nothing but the methods of the science of physics in his research.

"I am sure that you all realize why I have made this analysis of planning and organization in the physical world. In all living organisms we have highly complex structures, and when we can make actual investigations of structural details, we find in most cases the most intricate internal motions. An organism may be undeveloped and dormant, as in the form of a seed or an egg cell, but all the marvelous characteristics of the full-grown plant or animal must exist in potential form in the fertilized germ cell. As I have told you before, it has recently been found that all living organisms are imbedded in complex electrical fields, and the investigators claim that it is difficult to avoid the conclusion that the fields are the *cause* and not the *effect* of the organization. These fields disappear at death when ordinary physical forces can have a free play. It seems to me that such 'living fields' may be the mechanism by which the material in a growing embryo may be organized.

"But behind these organizing fields there must be an intelligence far surpassing our own. Our own body and its organs are not the result of any conscious thinking on our part, therefore I believe that the structure of an animal or a tree is no more the result of any conscious activity of the organism than the arrangement of the printer's ink in a book is the result of a consciousness in the ink. But the marvelous wisdom displayed must come from somewhere, and what is more natural than to identify this source with that cosmic source in which our own intelligence is rooted. In this way we can arrive at the idea of a God working *within* nature, yet not bound by the supposedly irrevocable laws of physics, and we arrive at it by looking for the *significance* of the facts we observe.

"As the physicist determining the properties of the paper and the ink in a book finds that the physical laws are applicable on every page in the book, so a biologist finds in his methods of investigation that physical laws are applicable everywhere in a living organism. But when the physicist starts to *read* the book, he finds that, even if it were a textbook in physics and written by the most thoroughgoing mechanist, the content of the book could not be accounted for by any physical laws at all, and that the book speaks to him as if it were an intelligent being. Similarly, when a biologist starts to *read* the book of nature instead of simply investigating it, he may find that it has a language of its own, and the ideas conveyed to him cannot be regarded as a product of his own mental idiosyncrasies. It may not be easy reading, and different people may not agree on the correct interpretation of the text. I think, however, that we agree that the text *has* a meaning and, if so, this meaning must be of extreme importance to all of us, since the significance of the human life is itself involved.

"The problem raised by Nelson now appears in a new light. Let us assume that there is an ultimate cause of all things and also of the rules that govern all natural phenomena, including those in our own mind. Since this ultimate cause is also the cause of our own consciousness, it must have an intelligence and a will, and we can therefore call it God. Some of these rules are apparently introduced once and for all, and we can identify them with the unchanging rules of physical science. Our will cannot modify these rules except within those parts of our own bodies which have nerve connections with the cortex of our brain. We can, however, act on other conscious beings by influencing their will, as when an officer orders a group of soldiers to advance. We have no direct evidence of our will being able to act on inorganic matter or on living organisms with a consciousness on a much lower level than our own.

"I do not claim that such effects are impossible, but as long as we have no clear evidence for them, we must leave them out of our consideration. Our own mind is, as we have shown, in intimate contact with its origin, which we have called God. Prayers to God are therefore significant, but I do not believe that God would suspend physical laws to satisfy our whims. I can by signs or by reasoning induce a man to do certain things, but this is not the only method of influencing his mind

Immortal Soul and Almighty God 187

and making him do something. A man in hypnotic sleep, in which state his own will power is weakened and his mind is abnormally receptive for the activities in the mind of a particular individual, performs acts in accordance with the will of the latter and the effect can be transmitted over large distances, and the transmission is independent of the distance. This fact can be regarded as a strong indication of all minds being in potential contact with one another, either directly or, what is more probable, through their roots in a universal mind.

"My answer to Nelson is therefore that no man can set a limit to the power of our minds. We certainly can influence the minds of other people by methods that cannot be classified as physical, or at least they cannot be included in the science of physics of the present time. By influencing other people's minds we can change the course of human events which, after all, are to us the most important. I believe that by the strong mental efforts of the good peoples of the earth, the evil forces in the minds of other men can be suppressed, and other forces can be made effective. The efficacy of prayers of the highest type lies, I think, not in any eventual success in changing the plans of God, of which we can know nothing at all, but in the strengthening and assertion of our own God-given powers to promote and to realize divine ideals high above the level of our animal instincts and desires."

Anderson replied, "I know nothing about the ultimate origin of consciousness or of anything else, and I doubt that anybody knows it. In regard to the first part of your statement I must emphasize that if we want to study the secrets of life, we must first investigate its details, otherwise our interpretations would be very superficial. Further, as you well know, the development of new species and new organs can be explained as a gradual process in which accidentally produced desirable qualities are retained in the struggle for existence of the race."

"It is quite true," said Berman, "that most of the symbols of which I spoke must be studied by appropriate physical and chemical means before they can be interpreted. Some symbols, however, are printed in large, bold type and their meaning is so obvious that any child can understand it. With regard to new organs being started by accidents, I do not subscribe to the view held by most biologists. A little modification in the structure of an animal may be retained in the race if it is useful and not harmful, but in most cases an organ is a very complex structure, that can serve a useful purpose only after it is completely developed. It should be obvious that a few feathers or a little flap of skin on the forelegs of a lizard does not give him ability to fly and thus escape his enemies. An eye or a system of eyes is of no use without the nerve cells we call optic ganglia. It is in nerve cells and in the almost inconceivably complicated nerve systems that we most clearly see the handwriting of a supreme intelligence that organizes the matter in an animal. It is very significant that it is this part of the writing in the book of nature that is associated with mental activities.

"The significance of the smaller type in the script of nature may easily be overlooked. We may study in detail the growth of a cell or an organism, but the significance of the very fact that there *is* a growth and that this growth is associated with extremely complex structural changes may be overlooked in our description of the processes. A mechanist watching a man writing a meaningful sentence is apt to forget that there are non-physical forces that ultimately determine the motions of the pen. I want particularly to call your attention to the existence of a conservation of structural details in the organizing fields, a conservation that makes it possible for such fields to retain many of their characteristic properties during millions of years of organic development. These fields can exist in an extremely concentrated and potential form in the egg cell, they expand to a moderate size in the embryo, reach their full size in the full-grown animal, and then contract and disappear at death.

"Perhaps the most remarkable thing is that an organizing field can contract and disappear, and a completely new type of organizing field begins to expand, producing a complete reorganization of all the cells in the animal. Such a marvelous transformation occurs, for instance, when a larva changes into a butterfly. Such things are significant, but they are easily forgotten when our attention is concentrated on the changes themselves, instead of on the causes that produce the changes. Life seems to be a hierarchy of well-separated field units. Starting from the fields in the individual cells, we have then the fields in the organs, and the more general field that is responsible for the organization in the animal as a whole. The structure of this field has a purpose, but no biologist can admit this. As von Brücke once said: 'Teleology is a lady without whom no biologist can live. Yet he is ashamed to be seen with her in public.'"

Boris had listened attentively to the discussion. For him it was one of the most thrilling experiences he had ever had. At first he had unhesitatingly agreed with the opinion of the biologist, but Berman's clear exposition of his views started a new line of thought in Boris' fertile brain. The idea of life as a symphony built of simple tones combined into accords came back to him, but he realized well that such an idea had little scientific value. When he heard Berman speak about field units governing the growth of living organisms, the field units expanding during growth and contracting and disappearing at death, new thoughts began to take shape.

Boris knew more about physics than about biology, and he asked himself now whether there were not in the inorganic world any well-defined field units that expanded and contracted. He had seen musical accords as wavy lines on an oscillograph, but these accords were man-made. What would be the appearance of a musical accord produced by a radiating atom? Was not radiation a kind of harmonic vibration emitted by the atom? This radiation sometimes appeared as highly concentrated elements of energy, the photons, but the photons did not travel like particles, but like waves. These waves retained their individuality during their motion, Berman had said, and then suddenly they appeared as small photons, that actually did the work. Without hesitation he described his ideas, formulating his thoughts as he went along.

"Some weeks ago we saw an experiment showing the interference of light, and we heard about the corpuscular and the wave nature of matter and radiation. Dr. Berman told us that we could not even apply the idea of motion to photons and electrons. We were told that the wave systems of photons have an individuality of their own, so that they never got mixed up with other photons, and that they could retain their identity during millions of years. It seems to me that these strange phenomena can be explained as the expansion of a distinct field element with definite and unchanging properties. These phenomena may well be of the same type as those manifested in living organisms, as Dr. Berman has just described for us. It is generally agreed that when an atom emits light, an electromagnetic wave system of a definite energy content is emitted, and this system can be described as an expanding wave front with a certain thickness. The strange thing is that when this extended wave system comes into contact with an exceedingly small atom of a particular type and in a particular state, the *total* energy of the extended wave system is absorbed by the atom.

"The wave system at the moment of absorption therefore acts as an exceedingly small particle, which is called a photon. This process can therefore be pictured as a contraction of a field unit, whereas the emission of light must be pictured as an expansion of the same field unit. The fact that a photon can only interfere with itself, and not with other photons, even if these are of exactly the same type, is analogous to the behavior of living cells, the organizing fields of which act as units, that is, one part of a cell cannot ordinarily be added to a part of another cell. In the case of radiation, the expansion proceeds with the speed of light, whereas the contraction must be instantaneous, and I admit that it is difficult to conceive of a physical process that is really instantaneous. In living organisms the expansion of the organizing, electrical field proceeds at a slow rate during growth and embryonic development, whereas the contraction at death is a relatively rapid process. Although the rate of change in size of the radiation field differs enormously from that in the organizing fields, the property of expansion and contraction seems to be common to both kinds of fields."

Berman had followed Boris' speech with extraordinary attention and in his creative mind new ideas were taking form. After a short silence he said, "Boris has called our attention to a very important analogy between radiation and living fields. They are both observable as complex electromagnetic fields, the former is not associated with matter and travels with a very high and definite speed, whereas the latter is associated with special kinds of matter and can only move at a relatively low speed, Living fields have a structure of extreme complexity and an extraordinary, inherent stability. Using Boris' analogy between life and music we may say that a living field represents a symphony in which the accords are bound together into a harmonious whole, so organized that each of the accords performs a special function essential for the harmony and the purpose of the whole symphony. A musical symphony has a rather loose type of organization, and it consists of a *sequence* of accords, whereas in a living symphony the interrelated accords are arranged side by side. In the 'overture' to the living symphony, represented by embryonic development of an animal, there is also a sequence of accords, some pointing to the past and others to the future of the race, and some occurring in the early and others in the later parts of the overture.

"The radiation from an atom is in the form of small individual electromagnetic field units, which ordinarily do not interact with one another. These elements have therefore a certain resemblance to living cells of an extremely simple type, but we have no right to regard them as living, since we cannot change our definition of life simply to suit our own fancies. But it seems to me quite possible that the electric fields associated with a living cell and responsible for its structure and functions can become completely detached from the atoms. Such a field cannot stand still, but must travel, presumably with the speed of light, to other places on the earth or in the universe. If conditions on another planet are suitable for life and if the proper kind of molecules are present, these traveling living fields may well be captured, and living protoplasm and even highly organized animals can thus be formed.

"It is interesting to note what happens when a photon is emitted by an atom. We know now that it does not move as a point but as an expanding wave system. If the wave system is not absorbed by another atom, and if we wait some thousands of years, this single field unit may have an enormous extension. Nevertheless, when it is finally absorbed, the whole amount of energy and momentum it carries is instantaneously absorbed by a single atom. Our ordinary ideas of space are completely inadequate to describe such a process. We can go one step further and picture the photon in transit as being submerged in a world to which our ordinary ideas of space and time are not applicable, that is, a world beyond that described in the science of physics. When the photon again becomes observable, it therefore seems to emerge from a non-physical world in the form of a certain amount of energy which has definite effects on the nerve cells in our eyes and on the sensitive grains in a photographic plate.

"If we apply this idea to living fields we conclude that life and mind can free themselves from any association with matter, that they then disappear into a world beyond the physical world, and that they can reappear in their original form and associated with new atoms. The last happens inside our brain, when mental functions are transferred from one part of the brain to another. This is not as strange as it sounds, since the atoms in our brain are continuously replaced by new ones, the old ones being removed as waste products. Our life and our mind are not anchored in any particular atoms in our body and in our brain. Our bodies may be compared with complex fields through which a current of matter is flowing from birth to death, a current which furnishes the building material and the energy we need in our daily life. My personality is not in the atoms of my body, or in the living field in which it is imbedded. It belongs to a world to which no reference is made in the textbooks of physics and biology."

"That is too deep for me," said Anderson. "If I understand you right you believe in Arrhenius' theory of panspermia, small organisms which are supposed to travel in interstellar space and can transmit life from one planet to another, and I have no particular objection to this theory. Whether the panspermia travel in the form of small particles or as wave systems may not be important, although I insist that they must be associated with matter when traveling through space. But I do not see how this can have anything at all to do with the immortality of the soul which we are supposed to discuss."

Berman spoke up. "I think there is a very intimate connection. Let me explain where the human soul comes in. We defined the human soul as the ego of man, a perceiving, willing, feeling, thinking, and remembering unit. I want particularly to emphasize the importance of memory. Our memory is a thing which makes us feel that our personality has been retained from childhood to old age. If we express memory in physical terms, we must imagine that in our brain we have some imprints of past events, imprints which can be stimulated by various means, and they then appear in our consciousness as memories of past events. These memory elements cannot reside in the atoms of the brain, since the atoms of the brain are all renewed in a relatively short time. The imprints mentioned must therefore be in the *field* of the brain, the field which gives the brain its complex structure, and not in the incorporated atoms and molecules. These imprints in the brain field must be extremely stable, since they can remain unchanged during a long lifetime, and they are not even destroyed by the penetrating cosmic radiation to which our brain is contin-

Immortal Soul and Almighty God

uously exposed and which is more intense than the radiation in the very center of an exploding atomic bomb.

"The memory field must be an essential part of the general brain field. In our memory field there are many elements of which we normally have no knowledge, but they can be brought up to the level of our consciousness by an unusually intense stimulation. It has been shown that during hypnotic sleep it is sometimes possible to recall in the greatest detail past events of our life, details of which we normally have not the slightest conscious knowledge. The stimulation of our brain seems to be brought about by oxidation of brain tissue, and after the destruction of certain nerve cells, the brain field, which is not modified by the destruction, soon restores the original structure of the brain cells. In order to stimulate a memory element we must therefore burn up the corresponding part of our brain.

"Our bodies are continually dying; every second some cells in our body die and others are born. This process is modified in our brain, where new cells cannot be formed by division and therefore must exist in potential form in the embryo and also in the egg cell. Memories probably cannot be associated with any particular nerve cells. Like thinking, they cannot be located in any isolated part of the brain. Instead they seem to be associated with the brain field as a whole. When a man dies, his brain field contracts and his brain disintegrates quickly, since its structure is no longer sustained by its organizing field. This field contains all the memories of the man, his soul, if you want to call it so. Where does it go to? Like the other fields of which we have spoken it goes to a world beyond space and time. It goes to the same world from where it originally came, the world where life itself has its origin. Since it has no longer any field structure, we should not call it a field at all, and the only name we can give it is a soul.

"Anderson said that the idea of a mind detached from matter is incomprehensible. Personally I think that a mind completely conditioned by atomic configurations and motions is even more incomprehensible. We do not think with the aid of complex molecules. It is very significant that our mental activities are associated with the oxidation of nerve cells, that is, when we *destroy* the structure our brain field has imparted to protein molecules. It is only when the molecules in our brain do not fit into the surrounding field structure that we are awake, when we can have sensations, and can feel, think, and remember. From this fact Bergson has concluded that the atoms in our brains are *obstacles* that prevent an avalanche of feelings, thoughts, and memories from descending upon our mind, all at the same time. The atoms form a screen or veil that makes it possible for us to concentrate on the immediate requirements of our earthly life. When this veil disappears at death, our memories from this and perhaps

Immortal Soul and Almighty God

from earlier lives crowd in upon us without hindrance, tormenting us or blessing us, and above all, teaching us about the real meaning of life. If Bergson is correct, and if we with life mean mental rather than physical development, then, when death comes, our real life begins anew."

After a short silence Nelson said, "This is all very interesting, but it is of importance only if it is true or partly true. I do not see how we can get any kind of scientific information about the kind of life you think exists after death and without any material body. I suppose you want to start a new science based on communication with departed spirits, but personally I do not want to have anything to do with it."

Berman smiled a little at his friend's remark when he said, "I do not know anything about departed spirits or how to communicate with them, but I think we all are in direct communication with a world beyond space and time. A thought is itself something that has no shape or size or other space properties, and it belongs therefore to a different world than that described in the science of physics. We are in contact with this nonphysical world when we think, feel, or will, and we are therefore quite familiar with this world beyond physics. In fact, we know much more about it than we know about the material world, the knowledge of which is based on shadows and not on substance, on rules but not on their meaning. I am convinced that we live in eternity now, but like an unborn child we are in deep sleep. Occasionally we have lucid moments when we realize that the world is not what it looks like. When we really wake up we may find eternity dimly spread out in front of us and our past clearly distinguishable behind us. Eternity beckons us to come on, but like young birds we are afraid to try our wings and plunge into the unknown, but mother nature kicks us out from our family nest to shift for ourselves. Mother nature knows what is best for us and cares little for our complaints and our agony."

"Don't run away from us so fast into an unknown world," said Nelson. "What you have said applies equally well to all animals with a consciousness and a memory. We cannot assign an immortal soul to man without doing the same thing to the higher animals. Do you really believe that your dog has an immortal soul and that he will suffer for eternity for having snatched a bone from another dog?"

Everybody smiled, but Berman was quite serious when he continued. "In order to answer this question we must first decide what we think is the purpose of life and of the universe as a whole. We all have a will governed by a purpose, and since we ourselves are parts or manifestations of Cosmos, the underlying power must also have a will and a purpose. I see this Cosmic Will in action everywhere and, above all, in my own mind. I realize well that certain actions of mine are of greater importance than others, that certain actions are trivial, whereas others may have an effect

Immortal Soul and Almighty God 201

among untold generations in the future. The killing of a fly is a trivial thing, but the deliberate killing of a friend may set an indelible mark on my memory. The life we see with our eyes is a system of transient symbols of a life in another realm where there is no death. Animals and plants have their roots in this realm, and when they die, their roots remain alive and may sprout again. Sir James Jeans claims that the atoms themselves have their roots in a world beyond space and time, and I think he is right.

"I have no doubt that man is an element in the universe more important than the animals and the plants and the atoms. Man is an animal in the mind of which some of the more fundamental properties of Cosmos are manifested. These properties or faculties are usually dormant but, when properly stimulated, they can be developed within an individual and among a race to a height to which we can set no limit."

Anderson appeared quite amused at Berman's pronouncement. He said, "If Bergson is correct, the best thing we can do is to commit suicide, for then we can learn many things which we are unable to grasp with a brain clogged up by atoms. I admit that nerve cells must be stimulated before they can act or before we can have any sensation or feeling, but this stimulation does not involve any actual destruction of nerve tissue, for if a nerve cell is completely destroyed it can never be regenerated. Further I do not relish the idea of having an avalanche of feelings and memories descending upon my mind. A little at a time is quite enough for me."

Berman realized well the importance of the biologist's remarks and he was quick to answer them. "We do not know exactly what happens to a nerve cell when it is stimulated, and we do not know at all how this stimulation can produce effects in our consciousness. But we know that in many cases the stimulation can be performed by mechanical or chemical means, and in whatever way the stimulation has been brought about, the effect in our consciousness depends solely on the specific nature of the nerve cell and not on the method used in its stimulation. Any mechanical or chemical action on the complex structure of a nerve cell represents a modification of the structure given to it by the living field of force which also retains and restores the structure. The interference is therefore not constructive but destructive, although the destruction is temporary and may not be very extensive. There can be little doubt that in the metabolism of the brain, nerve tissue is temporarily destroyed, and the metabolism is itself enhanced when the brain is abnormally stimulated.

"When our brain is not stimulated beyond the stage necessary for our organic life, we are asleep. From this fact it may be argued that an undisturbed brain field does not give us any sensations or feelings. This field must contain our memories in a potential form, and these must also be stimulated before they can appear in our consciousness. A potentiality that *never* becomes an actuality is of no importance, and its very existence can never be demonstrated. If our memory exists after death but is never stimulated, it can hardly be regarded as having any significance, at least not for the owner of the memory. But we must remember that many types of stimulation, like the association of ideas, cannot be regarded as mechanical, and who can tell about the many possibilities in this respect.

"I think we can safely rely on our instinct to use and to retain the capabilities we have in organic life. I have no doubt that we can use our brain to much better advantage than we usually do, and therefore I can see no reason to commit suicide. We have in our brain an instrument for direct communication with the cosmic consciousness. Ideas are attributes of Cosmos. For what else can they be? A combination of atoms cannot by itself produce a human thought. Cosmic ideas can be focused in any receptive brain, although the receiver may not be able to express them in understandable terms. Most ideas are trivial or incorrect, and their truth value must be carefully tested. Practically all of our ideas are highly colored by our own selfish desires, and it takes an exceptional man to forget himself and his personal interests in the search for eternal truths. Such truths have been incorporated in the intellectual heritage of the human race, and they act like a leaven that gradually turns our minds from animal hate and fear and selfishness into minds better fitted for the eternal life for which, I am convinced, we are all destined."

Boris felt a sudden exaltation at the last remarks by Berman. He had heard similar ideas expressed before, but his mind had always revolted against this kind of unrealistic philosophy, completely foreign to the world of ideas in which he had been brought up. Berman's philosophy reminded him of Spinoza's, but the former was more personal in its appeal than the austere intellectualism of Spinoza, where the individual appeared to be completely lost in the universal world substance. He felt that he was an active and important element in a meaningful world progress and not a passive, insignificant individual in a haphazard and meaningless evolution. He knew well that he could not satisfactorily explain his feelings, and he was afraid of sarcastic retorts from the scientists present. He therefore kept his thoughts to himself.

Davis had been following with great interest the exchange of views concerning the immortality of the soul and the indestructibility of memory, and he was obviously quite pleased with many of Berman's theories. "I have often heard it stated," he said, "that a soul is something completely beyond any scientific description or investigation, and that the notion of its survival at death is absurd or at least incompatible with sound, scientific thinking. I am therefore rather surprised and very glad to learn that a man well acquainted with modern science is ready to seriously consider the possibility of the immortality of the human soul and to present a picture of the physical processes involved.

"My own belief in this respect is not based on any scientific analysis, but on revelations given to the world by Jesus of Nazareth and by holy men inspired by God. Such revelations are not so absurd as they might seem. Did not Dr. Berman tell us that fundamental ideas can be focused in a human brain? We are all images of God, imperfect to be sure, but yet capable of understanding some of His attributes. I believe that Jesus, the carpenter from Nazareth, has better than any man expressed the meaning and purpose of human life. He told us to love God. As I understand it, this means that we should be in intimate and affectionate communication with God, the source of all things, and not let our selfish desires becloud our evaluation of ultimate realities and distort our sense of what is right and wrong. We then attain a harmony with the Cosmic Mind or Consciousness, or God, as I like to call it, a harmony that makes us happy even in adversity.

"I believe that we are all part of a bigger, cosmic life, and if we believe this, hate and fear disappear from our minds. Christ's commandment that I shall love my neighbor as myself becomes an obvious maxim, since all individuals on the earth are members of a higher organism in which the suffering and the rejoicing of the individuals are shared by all. It is easy to tell the state of ethical development of an individual or a nation by their attitudes towards their opponents. Christ's saying that we shall love our enemies is an expression for the attitude we should have as members of an all-embracing community of immortal souls. The commandment is contrary to all our animal instincts, but the very fact that it has been proclaimed at all and, to some extent at least, accepted shows that there are higher ethical standards than those to which we are accustomed. We can love the good in a man without condoning the evil in him.

"The theory of the indestructibility of memory interests me greatly. This means that a record is kept of all our actions, and we carry the record with us wherever we go. It says in the Bible that our deeds shall follow us, which is exactly the same thing. The very fact that we have a conscience is itself an important fact, although it is undeveloped among some individuals and highly developed among others. I am sure that our conscience will bring us happiness from our unselfish acts, but it will also bring suffering for our evil acts. But this suffering cannot be an end in itself; it would serve no useful purpose if it did not teach the suffering individual a lesson useful to him in the future.

"In Buddhist philosophy it is claimed that our souls finally lose their identity in a Nirvana, but only after they are thoroughly cleansed. It may well be so, but this is looking rather far into a future of which we have no knowledge. It does not seem unreasonable, however, since if we are parts of or emanations from God, we can presumably return to our original source when we have become properly adapted for an association of the highest order with this origin. This cleansing of our souls is supposed to require many reincarnations, and I do not feel competent to express any opinion about this theory."

There was a moment of silence and Wilson, the leader of the group, felt that the discussion had come to an end, and he made a few concluding remarks. "I am sure that we all feel that this has been a very interesting discussion. Although we may have quite different opinions about the problems discussed, we can all learn something by patiently listening to the presentation of conflicting views. As we must ascend from the valley to a high mountain to ascertain where we are and to survey the land around us, so we must ascend to high levels of thought before we can find out anything about our relationship with a wider world of which we feel instinctively that we are a part. Science has shown us that there are immutable rules that govern nature. But these rules do not apply to our thinking, for then we would be automatic machines and all discussion would be meaningless. When I say or write something, my will is the cause and not the effect of my actions, and will is therefore more fundamental than matter.

"In the living world we see with our eyes how a regulating agency links the past and the future by an intelligent action far beyond our understanding. This agency seems to emerge from the wider domain in which our own consciousness has its roots. Our mind is not fully our own, although we may mold it according to different patterns during our lives, and the molding is governed by our will, that has a certain degree of freedom. We appear to be gods on a small scale, and we can change our own destiny to some extent. Who can set a limit to what we can accomplish, if our will is in harmony with the Universal Will that governs everything? But if our will is not in harmony with the Cosmic Will, we may for a time retard our own development, and we recognize the conflict in our own suffering. I have no doubt that, in the long run, humanity will rise to high ethical levels, but we must all learn the required lessons. In order to learn these lessons properly we must be in intimate association with our 'teacher.' Most of our lessons consists of painful experiences, but when we look towards the goal, happiness returns to our soul.

"It is now pretty late, and I think we must conclude this interesting and pleasant meeting of 'The Searchers.' Perhaps in the future we can continue our discussions. The world is changing rapidly these days, and new facts are discovered at an amazing rapidity. Perhaps it may not be so long until we are able to see more clearly through the mist that hides so much of nature as well as our own destiny."

CHAPTER 9

Conversation in a City of Sleepwalkers

When leaving Dr. Wilson's apartment Boris followed Berman on his way out. It was a fine night, and the air felt very refreshing. They agreed to walk home, in spite of the large distances in the great city. Boris had many questions to ask, and Berman knew well that the young man was eager to explore the new vistas of thought that had been opened to his searching mind.

"I can't believe that there is a life after death," said Boris. "Has not science shown that any conscious activity requires a brain? A brain is built of atoms, therefore consciousness is dependent upon matter. An empty skull has no brain, and therefore no consciousness, and no soul. What is left of a man after death is often nothing but dry bones."

"Did you ever ask yourself what a thought or a memory is?" Berman asked. "They have no shape, no weight, and no physical properties, and they therefore belong to a different world than your skull and your bones. Your brain is an instrument by which you communicate with this other world, and this instrument has a recording mechanism where a record is kept of your transactions. This record is not in the atoms or the molecules of your brain, which are scattered at your death and form new chemical combinations and may even appear in the brain of another man or animal. You may say that the record is in the field that organizes the atoms in your brain, but this field is itself an idea in your own mind. In this way you come back to your own mind as the ultimate reality, all other things being fleeting but significant shadows. We cannot seriously believe that our ability to think, to plan, and to remember is a result of an originally accidental and later inherited concatenation of atoms in our brains. Our conscious activities must have a more fundamental origin, and to describe this origin we must have recourse to analogies taken from a world more familiar to us.

"An engineer is inclined to describe the universe as a machine, and any man who, like yourself, has been brought up in a materialistic and utilitarian world is apt to think of the universe in terms of an active struggle for food and material comfort. This is what Karl Marx did, and I suppose you are quite familiar with his teachings. But we do not need any elaborate philosophical system for its description; any animal is familiar with it, although he does not express it in words or perhaps not even in conscious thoughts. A poet or an idealistic philosopher may try to look deeper into the nature of things than does the materialist, and he looks for the significance of events and of his feelings, which he regards as symbolic of more fundamental realities than those described by the men of science. Intuitively he feels that there are more important things than atoms, and that there are eternal values that are not expressed in the mathematical equations of theoretical physics or in the textbooks of the economists."

"That may be all right, but it does not prove that there is a God or that I have an immortal soul," said Boris.

"Of course not," said Berman. "Nevertheless it gives you an idea that can form the basis for a scientific analysis of these beliefs. The record in your brain of which I spoke is a mechanical analogy introduced to remind us that our memories are preserved in some form and can be reproduced at a later time, and they can serve to identify a particular soul. The world in which our consciousness has its roots gives us a general idea of the nature of a God. As there is a conservation law of energy, of momentum, and of electric charge, so there seems to be a law of conservation of memories. Memory is that element in our consciousness that connects the past with the present. If we had no memory, there would be only one moment of our life, the moment we call *now*, and we would never consciously recognize more than this single moment. Here we have the analogy to our difficulty of recognizing the existence of any other life than our present. But even with a limited range of memory we can realize that the earth has existed before there were any conscious beings on the earth and will exist after the human race has vanished from its surface. Similarly, with our limited memory we can well visualize the existence of a personal memory with periods of higher and lower states of awareness of its own content.

"With regard to the existence of a God I want to call your attention to the fact that science has found that the material universe has uniform properties and it cannot be divided into mutually independent parts. All physical laws are interrelated, and they are apparently the same in all corners of the universe. Some aspects of this uniformity are undoubtedly a result of the uniformity of the human mind and therefore of our thinking, but there are also phenomena in which our mind plays the role of an observer. As an example of the latter type of phenomena I can mention the observed fact that atoms emit radiant energy in very small but definite amounts, quantitatively governed by a universal constant, the quantum of action. In biology a large number of phenomena have been discovered which cannot be deduced from any knowledge prior to the observed facts of nature. The fact that cells undergo division, for instance, cannot be deduced from our knowledge of atoms.

"If our mind has its roots or essence in a universal mind, it is not at all difficult to understand that at death it sinks back to the level of its origin. This level differs from the physical level by the fact that its manifestations do not take place in the framework of space and time with which the human mind is so familiar. This non-physical world is not a distant world, it touches every cell in our body and in our brain. Every time you feel, or think, or remember, you are actually working on this non-physical level.

"But an intelligence and a will beyond ourselves are almost impossible to conceive without a *bearer* of these faculties. An *impersonal* nature capable of intelligent thinking, and with a will of its own, is an absurdity to my way of thinking. In this way we are led to the belief in a Supreme Being acting intelligently and with a definite purpose. The undeniable fact that man has a conscious will, coupled with our conviction that this will must have an origin, is in my opinion the strongest scientific argument for the assertion that there is a God and that our life has a meaning.

"The trouble with us is that we are asleep most of the time. Like an unborn child we do not know that we are alive and that we have great potentialities. After we are born we have lucid periods when we realize that there is a world around us, that things happen according to definite rules, and that we are members of a society of beings very similar to ourselves. I am convinced that if we could really wake up, we would find ourselves being parts and parcels of an all-embracing universe. I also believe with Bergson that it is the matter in our brain that keeps us asleep, and to regain consciousness we must to some extent free ourself from this impediment. We have important work to do right now, but if we are asleep we cannot do it. I often feel as if I would like to rub my brain a little to find out what is the real meaning of my life. If I have a role to play in the cosmic drama, I want to play it as a man and not as a machine. As I see it, it is this very desire for conscious knowledge which shows that I am more than a machine and that I am prepared to accept certain responsibilities for my actions."

Boris stopped suddenly in his walk with a startled expression on his face. He remembered his dream about the genie in his brain who wanted him to burn up the brain and set him free. He told Berman about this strange dream he had had about a month earlier.

Berman was greatly interested and said: "You saw things more clearly in that dream than you have ever done in your waking state. It was your subconscious mind that was working, a mind that probably never sleeps and has a logic of its own, and it can sometimes penetrate the veil that separates appearances from reality. As usual your thinking took a symbolic form, and the symbols were taken from a world familiar to you, and then you applied them to a less familiar world. This is what we always do when we describe unfamiliar things."

"What do you think is the real meaning of our lives?" asked Boris. "A man seems to me a very small and trivial thing, and I do not see how he can play any important role in the cosmic drama of which you spoke."

"We may be small, but I am sure we are not trivial elements in the cosmic plan," said Berman. "You are more important than the biggest star or the largest star system in the universe. You have a consciousness that can encompass the whole universe, its past, its present and, to some extent, its future, and I doubt that any star can do that. Inorganic fields are much simpler than living fields, and the most complex of these fields are those in the human brain. If complexity can be regarded as a criterion for importance, the human brain is the most important thing of which we have any knowledge.

"We all know that there are many people who do not seem to amount to anything, and there are people who do not seem to have risen much from the animal level. A new-born child is in many respects very similar to an animal, yet it can develop into a being with very high intelligence. If properly trained, a savage can learn many things, and his children or grandchildren can successfully compete with individuals of what we have been used to regard as more intellectual races.

The human mind has the most astonishing adaptability, and it is impossible to set a limit to the intellectual heights it can reach. But much more important than the intellectual level is the ethical level he will attain. What good does it do a man if he knows all the secrets of the universe, but does not apply his knowledge to the betterment of his own soul or to the welfare of his fellow men? The betterment of a man's soul results in a harmony irrespective of the conditions of his life, a harmony that only a clear conscience can give to a man."

"But there are many people who do not seem to have any conscience at all," said Boris. "Hitler felt that he had an important mission to fulfill, and as long as everything went well, he probably felt that he lived a happy life. I do not think he was ever bothered about the suffering he caused."

"There was nothing wrong with Hitler's impulse of improving the standard of living among the German people. But the methods he used called for the subjugation and slavery of other people, and therefore the results were evil. There is nothing wrong with a man's love for his family, but if he kills other people to further the interests of his loved ones, his intentions can no longer be regarded as good. A love that is not universal is very often a form of selfishness and must be condemned. Wise men through the ages have understood this. Religious men express this by saying that 'God is Love,' and that His love extends to all living things. I will go so far as to say that love is a more potent weapon than an atomic bomb. I do not think we are ready for this more potent weapon yet, but we can at least tell everybody about its great powers, so that all the peoples of the world can use it. It should never be kept in hiding as a secret weapon."

They had arrived at the house where Berman lived. A handshake, a "goodbye," and a "good luck," and Boris was alone.

Boris walked home. The city's many lights were shining brightly, there were automobiles in the streets and pedestrians on the sidewalks, in spite of the late hour. There was happiness and sadness all around him, and for the first time he felt that his own happiness depended upon the happiness of fellow men completely unknown to him. At the same time he felt himself to be a very important person, wide awake in a city peopled by sleepwalkers, and this feeling gave him a sense of exultation. He saw the ocean of eternity right in front of him, and it challenged him to come out and try his powers. Its dark waves did not frighten him, for he was himself a son of eternity, and among these waves was his real home. He saw the whole universe mirrored in his mind, and clearly he saw an austere face wherever he looked. But compassion and love were mixed with the austerity, and an expression of great joy was mingled with the dark shadows of the miseries of the world.

"It is a great world," he said to himself. "It is too

bad that this world may be destroyed in a future war. But can I do nothing to save it? I think I will rub my brain tonight. When the genie appears, I shall ask him to help me. If he can't do that, I shall ask him from where he derives his power. When I have learned that, I shall communicate with this higher authority."

"That's what I shall do," said Boris.

Epilogue

The Immortality of the Human Soul; A Scientific Approach

THE IDEA of the immortality of the human soul is very old. Nearly all mythologies contain assertions that the human soul survives at death, in itself a strange fact since it is not borne out by any direct evidence. In the Chinese, the Indian and the Greek philosophies the immortality of the human soul is taken almost for granted, although different opinions are expressed about its individuality in a future existence. The immortality of the human soul is a fundamental element in Christian theology, and without this doctrine Christianity would be little more than a set of ethical rules. Most of the believers in these religious creeds maintain that this doctrine has developed from an intuitive knowledge acquired by inspired men, a knowledge that cannot be based on logical reasoning and must be accepted on faith alone.

Modern man is in general more critical than were his ancestors. Experience has taught him that many of the beliefs of earlier times are untenable, in spite of the fact that they were once generally accepted and even regarded as self-evident. Critical men of the present time look to science with its established facts, research methods and cool reasoning for an unbiased judgment. But science has not given the religious man any encouragement in his belief in the immortality of the human soul. On the contrary, biologists claim that when an organism dies, nothing is left but the material of which it was built, and that this material may enter into new chemical combinations and be incorporated in other organisms. It is also claimed that consciousness can only be associated with matter in the form of nerve cells, and that when these are destroyed at death, the consciousness of the individual is lost forever. In other words, a feeling, a thought or a memory, not associated with a nervous system and a brain, is something unknown to science and contrary to all scientific evidence. Since the human soul can be defined as the perceiving, feeling, willing, thinking and remembering ego in man, and since this entity, whatever it may be, cannot perform its functions after the death of the body, we must conclude that it is annihilated at death.

This was the almost unanimous verdict of the scientists of the last century, and it is still the most common opinion among scientific men. During the last forty years, science—and particularly physical science—has developed in new directions, and the mechanical concepts of the last century have been

Epilogue

found to be inapplicable. The relativity theory and the quantum theory, which are based on well-established facts, have taught us that our so-called common sense can lead us astray, and that nature is not built on the lines envisaged by the scientists a generation ago. Philosophers long ago told us that the world of which we have any immediate knowledge is a world of fleeting phenomena in our consciousness, and that the substance of the external world eludes all physical investigations. Prominent scientists of the present time have proclaimed that the physical world is a pragmatic construct of our mind, very useful in many ways, but that it is limited to a description of structures and their relationship in space and time. Because of this critical attitude of modern science, the old idea that atoms and matter are themselves products of the type of perception, imagery and thinking characteristic of the human mind has again been given serious consideration.

Thoughts and memories are the most important characteristics of the human soul as we have defined it. An analysis of the problem of the immortality of the human soul must therefore involve a study of the nature of thoughts and memories and of their relationship to the brain with which they are known to be associated. Our brain has properties similar to other living structures, and before we can tell anything about what happens at death, we must first study the nature of life. Let us therefore ask the question what it is that distinguishes living matter from dead matter.

In order to emphasize an important characteristic of life I shall tell a parable. A Bedouin was riding on his camel in the desert. A strong wind came up and the dust started to blow. He dismounted and took refuge behind the animal and watched the sand being whirled around by the gusty wind. He saw a column of dust approaching, and it seemed to have the shape of a man. Gradually the dust condensed into a human body, with two legs and two arms, a torso and a head. "That's a genie," the frightened Bedouin said to himself. The genie shook his newformed body and stretched his arms and legs. In a deep voice he greeted the Bedouin, extolled the powers of Allah, and began a discourse about the mysteries of life, the relationship of mind to matter, and the source of all evil. Then the genie disintegrated, and nothing was left but a heap of dust.

This description of the formation and disintegration of a man does not differ essentially from that given in our textbooks of biology. We are all built of the same kind of atoms as is everything else in the universe. There is something that organizes this material; something that produces organs with definite functions necessary for the life of our bodies as complete systems. This something must also be able to produce a nervous system with a brain capable of conscious activities. It must have definite parts, but it must also be a highly co-ordinated system. It must integrate our mental activities, with the result that we are not a colony of reacting cells, but unified personalities who will, and think and remember. When this organizing factor is lost, the matter of which we are built reverts to a more stable state which does not exhibit any evidence of purposeful activity.

What is it now that arranges the atoms and molecules in our bodies in such a way that they form a highly organized living system? In physics we speak about fields of force as determining the motions of bodies, and particularly the changes in their motions. Many of us have seen how a horseshoe magnet can arrange iron filings in rows extending from one pole to the other. Scientists do not attempt to explain how such effects are actually brought about, but simply describe the phenomena in the specific language of physics, and attribute them to a modification of the properties of the space in the neighborhood of the magnetic poles. It has recently been found that the properties of a field of force cannot be the effects of the electrically charged particles assumed to exist within the atoms. For instance, electrons do not, as formerly was assumed, move in orbits around the atomic nuclei or like bullets from one place to another. The field that determines the characteristics of the atoms and the propagation of electrons consists of oscillating elements and has properties similar to a system of waves, and these waves determine statistically where and when we can expect energy-carrying particles to make their appearance. It also follows that the fields which determine the structure and functions of a living organism are *autonomous*, that is, they are not determined by the configuration and motions of the atoms in the matter of which the organism is built.

Naturally we are puzzled by the stability and integrity of these autonomous fields, a stability so great that they can be retained in nearly unchanged form during millions of years, in spite of the fluidity of the incorporated matter. In a very interesting and thought-provoking little book entitled *What is Life?* (Macmillan, New York, 1946) the founder of modern wave mechanics, Erwin Schrödinger, has applied wave mechanical considerations to explain the stability of the fields governing the structure of living organisms. He compares the genes, the hereditary elements existing in the nuclei of the germ cells and reproduced in the body cells, with liquid, aperiodic crystals, which are relatively stable at ordinary temperatures. The structure of the genes in the germ cells is duplicated in the genes in the body cells, and the wave systems in the genes serve as governing and stabilizing centers in the formation of a living organism. The fixed structure of an organ, for instance, must then be regarded as the result of stabilizing factors in the nuclei of its cells. Such stabilizing effects are evident in the healing of wounds and the restoration and regeneration of damaged organs. Schrödinger claims that in order to understand the space-time aspect of life—its deeper aspects are according to him beyond human understanding—we must introduce physical laws different from the statistical laws on which modern physics is built. These laws must involve orderly interactions between the separated parts of a system, and the genes represent, in Schrödinger's words, "the finest masterpiece ever achieved along the lines of the Lord's quantum mechanics."

Schrödinger calls attention to the well-known fact that the size of an organism is not determined by its structure. As a drastic example he envisages a drone as a greatly enlarged spermatozoon. This independence of size is of fundamental importance in the present study. In several earlier publications I have described growth as an "expansion of a living field." (A description of such fields and references to the literature are given in an article "The Autonomous Field", published in 1945 by the Franklin Institute. Together with several other related articles it is reprinted in the new edition of the writer's *The Soul of the Universe*.) Schrödinger's analysis may be regarded as the beginning of a quantum-mechanical foundation of living fields. We can compare a living field with a melody. A musical melody is the effect on our organs of hearing of a time sequence of frequencies, and the melody is not changed if it is played fast or slow, forte or pianissimo, provided the frequencies and their order are unchanged. A field of force is a pattern of frequencies existing in *space* as well as in time. A living field can therefore be described as an intricate frequency pattern, a "symphony of life" that retains its properties when undergoing great changes in size. Its intricate physical properties indicate the existence of qualities of a type quite different from those described in the science of physics. Some of these qualities we shall later describe.

Biologists have direct evidence of expanding fields in living organisms. Hans Spemann, one of the greatest embryologists in Germany, introduced in 1921 the idea of "organizing fields" responsible for the organization during embryonic development. During this development a progressive "wave of organization" can be studied in the microscope as changes in the appearance of the cells, which all appear to have about the same latent potentialities, the field determining which of these potentialities will be developed in one part of the embryo and which in other parts. In the vertebrates the center from which the main organizing field seems to expands has been located in the dorsal lip of the socalled blastopore, the tiny opening of an embryo in its gastrula stage. (During this stage the outer cell layers are turned into the cavity of the embryo, a process that takes place in man and in practically all animals). In these animals the progress of the organizing field is observed as a formation of nerve tissue from which the spinal cord, the nervous system and the brain later develops. If we remove the small piece of an embryo mentioned above and transplant it in the cavity of another gastrula of the same kind of animal, the transplanted piece induces the formation of a secondary embryo at the place of transplantation, and the building material of the secondary embryo is furnished by the "host." If we make a constriction in the median plane of an embryo, we can produce an animal with two heads. If we retain the constriction for a longer time, we can produce two complete embryos from a single one. It is significant that such changes are facilitated by shaking the embryo, in which case we evidently destroy the close structural correspondence between the fluid cell material and the inherent structure of the organizing field, and the field can then more freely respond to external influences. The fact that a field of force, so complex that it can by itself determine the structure and the vital functions of a living animal and a living man, can be split into two parts, each of which is identical with the parent field, is of the utmost significance in our study. Three-dimensional physical space is unable to accommodate the innumerable details involved in this complex process, a process that does even involve the duplication of mental potentialities and faculties. What we observe with our eyes is evidently a *partial aspect* of a much more fundamental process.

Another biological discovery of great importance in our study must here be mentioned. It has been known for many years that the activities in muscles and nerves are associated not only with chemical changes but also with electrical phenomena in and around the muscles and the nerves. Starting from these facts Burr and Northrop of Yale University, proposed in 1935 the "electrodynamic theory of life." This theory induced Burr, Lane and Nims to construct a very sensitive microvoltmeter particularly suited for the study of the fine structure of the electric fields around living animals and plants. Working with this instrument, a group of research men of the Section of Neuro-Anatomy of the Yale Medical School has found that all living matter is imbedded in electrical fields, which have a complex, fine-grained and well-defined structure extending beyond the animals and the plants studied. During embryonic development the electric activity is most intense and extends well beyond the organism, and apparently furnishes a predetermined pattern which defines the future growth and transformations of the developing embryo. At death the "living field" disappears. The inorganic fields inherent in all matter can then freely act according to their nature, the result being a general disintegration of the complex fluid matter and the formation of simpler compounds. Burr, the leader of the research group, states that "it is hard to escape the conclusion that the electrical pattern is primary and in some measure at least determines the morphological pattern."

To a biologist this statement from a physicist sounds almost like heresy, because, if we accept his conclusion, it would be necessary to take into account vital factors in biology which are not determined by the properties of matter. But physicists need not be unduly alarmed because, as I have said before, the idea of particles as the direct cause of force fields has been found to be untenable. These form-producing fields are evidently identical with the "organizing" or "embryonic" fields of Spemann, and they form a nonmaterial latticework through which our food flows, part of which being temporarily retained and assimilated. Such living fields must be included in any theory of life and of mind, and they are indispensable for our understanding of the immortality of the soul.

We have defined the human soul as the perceiving, feeling, willing, thinking and remembering ego in man. These faculties are known to be associated with the brain, and we conclude that the soul is associated in some way or other with the brain. The structure of the brain can no more be the result of its chemical composition than can other organs of the body. It has long been known that the normal and the abnormal activities of the brain are to some extent manifested by electric waves, often called brain waves. Some of these waves are intimately associated with our vision and seem to be the physical manifestations of the framework in space and time in which we place our mental sensations of light and colors. When our field of vision appears to be blurred or swaying, it is this framework which is abnormally affected. All mental activities are probably associated with brain waves, but these are in general difficult to observe and to analyze, and a detailed correlation is therefore difficult to establish. Some experts claim that certain personality traits are reflected in the electric wave pattern of the brain.

The thing that identifies a soul is its memory content. If we had no memory, we could be aware of only one moment, *now*. We would be completely unaware of any existence prior to this moment, and everything that happened at a particular moment would be forgotten the next. We could not even learn about our existence prior to the present moment, since such information would have to be given us in the form of a sequence of connected ideas, and without memory such sequences cannot be formed by the mind. We all know that we can remember events that happened many years ago. Our memories cannot be imprinted in the atoms of our brains,

Epilogue

since new atoms are continuously incorporated in the brain, and the old atoms are removed as waste products, so that we have a "new" brain in a relatively short time. Memories must therefore be imprinted in or associated with the brain field, that is, the nonmaterial field of force that organizes and stabilizes the matter of which the brain is built. The brain field has developed from the human embryo, and we must assume that it existed in some potential form in the human egg cell. This brain field has expanded during our embryonic development, it has been modified by our experiences, and a record of our activities is preserved in the field. This record of our activities must have a very high stability since memory elements can remain unchanged during a long life, although we may have difficulty in activating them. Our memory is unaffected by the intense electric fields in the atoms of the brain, and it is not even destroyed by the cosmic radiation which penetrates the skull and is more intense than the radiation from an atomic bomb. It has been found that sense impressions of which we never have had any conscious knowledge are registered in our memory, and they can be brought up to the level of consciousness under abnormal conditions. It is very probable that *all* our sense impressions are registered permanently in our memory, although only a few of them are ever remembered consciously.

Let us now see what happens at death. When a

living organism dies, the field that determines its structure and functions disappears. Since all living fields are highly integrated and very stable, there is no reason for believing that it disintegrates; instead we must assume that it contracts and during its contraction retains its inherent structure and properties in a potential form. This contraction can be regarded as the reversal of the expansion during embryonic development, although the contraction in general is more rapid than the expansion, when work has to be done in assimilating and organizing the matter of which the organism is being built up. In some animals we have direct evidence of this gradual contraction. Sometimes it can be arrested, and the field can then be made to expand again, as when a shriveled up animal is restored to life. Sometimes an organizing field contracts and disappears, and a field of an entirely different type appears and reorganizes the cell material. This is what happens when a larva gradually changes into a butterfly. We can therefore safely assume that at death our brain field, on which our memories are indelibly "engraved," contracts in unchanged form and disappears from the physical world, that is, the world of matter, radiation and force fields which we describe by their structures in space and time.

What happens when the sphere of action of the brain field becomes nil? Perhaps it has a form of existence that cannot be described in the terms used

Epilogue

in the science of physics? I now assert that it disappears into a non-physical world from which it originally came, and that in describing its properties and activities we must use terms appropriate to that world.

Let me explain what I mean by a non-physical world. In the science of physics the properties of a field of force are derived from measurements of space and time intervals, and the measurements of different observers are related by the rules described in the Theory of Relativity. These measurements are usually given in terms of arbitrarily chosen units of length and time, but they can also be given as numbers expressed in atomic standards fixed by the electromagnetic properties of matter. Physical science is to a great extent a system of rules governing such numbers, and mathematics is therefore its proper language. But we are all well aware of another realm where the framework of space and time plays a great role, but not as numbers of this sort. The visualizations we make in our everyday life and in our dreams are projected on a framework of a space and a time which, unlike the space and time of the science of physics, are not dependent on one another, and they represent significant data, although they cannot be expressed by reproducible measurements. This "sensed" space and time belong to this other realm which I have called the *non-physical world*. It is often called a *mental* world, but this does not exclude its basic reality. The world of physics is conceived and to some extent constructed by our mind and is therefore itself mental, but nobody doubts its reality as an objective form. Non-physical space has topological but no fixed metrical properties, a fact manifested by the duplicable but sizeless field structures of the living world. A child or a savage knows almost as much about this space as does the most astute theoretical physicist or the most penetrating philosopher, even if the former do not write abstruse treatises on the subject. It is quite possible that *all* conscious beings have an innate sense of a separating space and of a progressing time.

In my book *The Soul of the Universe,* referred to above, I have given many reasons for the belief that organic life as well as our mental qualities and faculties have their ultimate origin in and are in unbroken communication with a non-physical world. The germ cells are the incipient indicators in the physical world of space and time of an underlying, non-physical essence, and they define, not the actual, but the possible locations of the emergent essence of life. During embryonic development the biologists observe this emergence as expanding, organizing fields of force, a development which is the observable manifestations of more fundamental processes occurring in the non-physical world. There lies also the ultimate origin of light and colors, of sound and music, of feelings and emotions, of will

Epilogue

and anticipation, of thoughts and ideas, as well as of our feelings of guilt, of remorse, and of bliss. The nerve cells in our nervous systems and our brains are the "gates" or "links" by the aid of which we are able to communicate with the non-physical world —and then we perceive the essence of the universe.

We have said that one of the most important characteristics of a human soul is its memory content. We have also said that this memory is inseparably associated with the brain field, but this statement must now be qualified in an important way. A field of force cannot by itself harbor or produce any conscious thoughts or memories, since these belong to the non-physical world. These thoughts and memories may temporarily become "chained" to a particular type of matter waves, and then they become effective as electromagnetic brain waves, which therefore can be regarded as the *physical manifestations* of activities in the non-physical world. The same is the case with our conscious and unconscious will which, although belonging to the non-physical world, can produce electric phenomena in our brains and nerves and thereby regulate mechanical processes in our muscles and our organs. Our real selves, our souls, belong before our birth, during our organic life and after our death to the non-physical world. During organic life our mental activities are effective on another plane, which the physicists describe as the four-dimensional space-time continuum. Due to the inertia in the physical world and the intimacy of the connections, this effectiveness is offset by a corresponding limitation of our inherent mental faculties and abilities. This type of activity, however, gives us unforgettable experiences, some pleasant but more often very painful, which seem to be a part of our spiritual development.

On the basis of these ideas let us see what kind of life we can expect after death. In the non-physical world to which we return at death, we can expect to find an ever-acting source of energy, an idea which in the Theory of Emergent Energy has made possible a reconciliation of the wave nature and particle nature of matter and radiation. We can also expect to find the essence of life, the physical manifestations of which constitute the subject matter of the science of biology. There is time, but a time without change is meaningless. Therefore we can expect changes, presumably a progress towards a definite goal which we can only dimly discern. Non-physical time cannot, like physical time, be measured by clocks or estimated by the immediately sensed periods of electromagnetic brain waves. In that world a second may appear as eternity, and eternity is not measured as a number of fixed time units. The linkages in non-physical time may be quite different from those in physical time, and the past may well be linked with the future in the same way as the future is linked to the past. (This peculiarity of non-physical time is of importance for our understanding of teleological phenomena in biology, the principle of least action in physics, determinism and free will, premonitions, as well as certain dreams in which a sudden external stimulation produces an essential climax to a long dream-story, ostensibly progressing in physical "brain time.") In the non-physical world, space means simply separation of individuals, in contradistinction to their fusion, but there are no standards by which we can measure such separations. This "separation" can be expected to be relative and discriminatory and based on spiritual affinities and aspirations. There is nothing that corresponds to an upper limit of velocity, like the velocity of light in the physical world. There are light and colors, but no electromagnetic radiation; there are sounds and music, but no elastic vibrations; there is pleasure and beauty, and there is pain and sorrow. Mental communication can be expected to be instantaneous and even in the reverse time direction, whatever be the sensed separation in space and in the forward or backward direction of time. All the memories of our last and our previous lives can be reviewed in full details in an instant, since there are no atoms which in the physical world block and slow down all our mental activities. The records and motives of any man may well be perceptible to any other man, and there can then be no deception. The effects of our good deeds are obvious to all, and so are the effects of our evil acts. The memories of the cruel acts we have committed against men and animals follow us through eternity. The victims of a tyrant are all there, and the memories of their suffering haunt their oppressor. The torment he suffers will probably produce a strong urge in his mind to make a new "emersion" into the physical world, partly in order to escape temporarily from the pangs of his conscience and partly to make an attempt to improve his record. (Such emersions occur in the egg cells of a certain type of mammals. These egg cells first appear as a special kind of microscopic "ripples" on the surface of space-time.) The good and highly developed men can be assumed to be quite happy in the non-physical world and feel no urge again to visit a place like the sorrowful earth. Some of them may perhaps be sent on missions to the physical world, and even if they may suffer at the hands of evil men, they are happy in the service of the *Inscrutable One*.

The picture here presented of the conditions in the non-physical world has a striking resemblance to the pictures of heaven and hell presented in many religious philosophies on earth. The picture given is, of course, to a certain extent conjectured, but the least we can say is that there is no conflict between modern science and the age-old ideas of a life after death with rewards and punishment for the individuals. Wise men through the ages have intuitively

Epilogue

grasped these fundamental ideas concerning the meaning of our lives. This is not surprising since thinking is a fundamental characteristic of the non-physical world, and our ideas are rooted in this world from which we all have come and to which we return at death. This world is not "up in the sky," it is right here and it touches every cell in our bodies, an idea familiar from modern geometry of many dimensions. The reason why we do not all receive these profound ideas is that we, like other animals, have our attention fixed on food, shelter and comfort, on defense against our enemies, on our pleasures, and on our petty vanities. Some of these things are essential for our daily life, but if we allow them to obstruct our vision completely, we behave like animals and not like men. In our mind there is a spark of a divine origin which, if not quenched by our selfish desires, may burst into a flame that can illuminate our field of vision and make it possible for us to discern vistas belonging to a greater world. We realize then that every man, from the humblest to the most exalted and from the most evil to the most Christlike, is a son of eternity. His real home is not on earth, but in another world where suffering is temporal, but hope eternal. This hope emerges in our mind from the greater world, and it brightens our everyday life and tells us that it is full of meaning. It serves as a beacon guiding man on his long road, from the cruelty, selfishness and fear arising from his animal instincts, to the compassion, unselfishness and confidence characteristic of a future life for which he is preparing himself.

>
> Behind the clouds are Milky Ways
> That dance in space and time
> To music that a master plays
> Inspired by love sublime.
>
> Behind the clouds—a wider scope
> For joy that always seems
> To interlace eternal hope
> With everchanging dreams.
>
> Sister Benediction.

Index

Action, Quantum of, xii, 50, 73
Alpha particles, 82
Atomic bomb, xi, 80ff
  energy, 80ff
  nucleus, 82, 84ff
  number, 91
  power, Renunciation of, 108
Atoms, xi, *passim*

Bergson, Henri, 161, 198
Bethe, H. A., 103
Biology, xii, 113ff
Blastopore, 113f, 226
Blastula, 113
Bohr, Nils, 83
Brain, 114, 120, 146ff
Bragg, Sir William, 47
de Broglie, Prince Louis, 64f
von Bruecke, E. W. R., 190
Burr, H. S., 130, 228f

Chance, 72
Christ, 44
Chromosomes, 113
Color sensations, 150f
Conscience, x, 170f, 216
Crystals, 63, 131
Cytoplasm, 113

Davisson, C. J., 63
Death, 231ff
Diffraction of electrons, 62ff
  of light, 48ff
Driesch, Hans, 121
Du Bois-Reymond, Emil, 146
Eddington, Sir Arthur, 20, 35
Egg cells, 113
Einstein, Albert, 29, 35, 50, 54
Electric fields, 75ff
Electromagnetic waves, 53f
Electrons, 63ff, 82ff, *passim*
  Positive, 87, 92

Embryonic development, 113, *passim*
Energy, xi, 37f, 74f, *passim*
Energy levels, 87f
Ether, xi, 29, 49
Ethics, x

Fields, Autonomous, xii, 78, 130, 224
  Electric, 75ff
  Gravitational, 37, 43
  Organizing, xii, 117, 130, 226
  Living, 124, 130ff, 159, 193f
  Expansion and contraction of, 189
  Independence of size, 225
Fission, Nuclear, 94f
Force, 31f
Force fields, xif, 41f, 77, 223
Fresnel, A. J. 49

Galileo Galileo, 32f, 174
Gastrula, 113f
Genes, 113, 224f
Genie, 140f, 218, 222
Germer, L. H., 63
Ghosts, 78
God, xi, xiii, 9f, 42ff, 129, 154, 168f, 205f, 211ff
Gravitation, 28ff

Heart, 116
Heaven, 238
Hell, 238
Hormones, 123f
Huygens, Christiaan, 49
Hydrogen, 83f

Idealism, x
Ideas, 203
  Platonic, x

Index

Immortality of human soul, xiii, 166ff, 219ff
Inertia, 34f
Interference of light, 46f, 51ff
Iron, 18
Iron atoms, 91f

Jeans, Sir James, 77
Jesus of Nazareth, 23, 205

Knowledge, 69
Subconscious, x

Lavoisier, A. L., 30
Leibnitz, G. W., 155
Love, 106, *passim*

Marx, Karl, 210
Mass, 34f, 39ff
Mass number, 91
Materialism, x
Matter and mind, xiii, 145ff
Memory, 196ff, 211f, 230f, 235
Metaphysics, xiv, 14
Metaphysians, 14, 24, 38, 56
Mind and matter, xiii, 145ff
Minkowski, H. 54
Motion, 39f, 57f, 61f, 69
Mysticism, 14

Natural science, xiv
Nature, 10, 180
Neptunium, 94
Northrop, F. S. C., 228
Nerve cells, 26, 152ff
Optic, 150ff
Origin of, 157
Neutrons, 85f, 91ff
Newton, Sir Isaac., 28, 48
Notochord, 114
Nuclear fission, 94
Numbers, 20

Objects, ix
Observer, 73
Organization, 181ff
Organizers, 124

Particles, Annihilation of, 103
Perception, 60
Phenomena, x
Photons, 51ff, 122, 191

Planck, Max, xii, 23f, 50
Plato, x
Plutonium, 95f
Positrons, 92
Prayers, 186f
Protons, 83f, 91ff

Quantum of Action, xii, 50, 73

Realists, ix, 14
Relativity, Theory of, xi, 35, 39
Religion, 10
Russia, 43, 177
Rutherford, Lord, 82

Schrödinger, E., 224f
Science, Natural, xiv
Sensations, 150
Sense organs, 17, 20
Shadows, 15ff, 58, *passim*
Single-crystals, 63
Societies, Human, 164f
Soul, Human, x, 166ff, 220ff
Immortality of, xiii, 166ff
Space, 69
Non-physical, 233f
Space-time, 40f, 43, 235
Spemann, Hans, 117, 125, 226, 239
Sperms, 113, 121
Spinoza, B. 8f, 42, 155, 204
Structure, 18
Substance, 55, 78
Sun, 13f, 103
Symphony of life, 125f, 132f

Teleology, 182, 190
Time, 69
Non-Physical, 233f

Uncertainty Principle, 73
Uranium, 94ff
Source of power, 104f

Verne, Jules, 34
Viruses, 132f
Voltaire, François de, 178

Water, Heavy, 100f
Waves, 68
Will, 42, 116, 207, 213, 235
Cosmic, 208, 213
World, Non-Physical, 199ff, 233ff